Rouge Hags

Behind The Cosmetics Counter

Marlit Polsky

*To Gunita, dear
Love,
Marlit*

ISBN 978-0-9898232-1-0

Book Design
Ron Humphrey

Cover Design
Gunter Stern

Windjammer Adventure Publishing
289 South Franklin Street, Chagrin Falls, OH 44022
Telephone 440.247.6610 Email windjammerpub@mac.com

DEDICATION

To my children

Richard

Mark

Jill

My objective in writing this memoir is to entertain the reader and to chronicle my experiences in the retail beauty business.

ACKNOWLEDGEMENTS

Gunter Stern—New York award winning artist—Thanks for the book cover.

Richard Polsky—Thanks for the support and encouragement.

Margi Zitelli—Thanks for editing.

Co-workers—Thanks for cheering me on.

CONTENTS

INTRODUCTION

"Good morning, Rouge Hags!"

My co-workers didn't necessarily embrace my "cheeky" chosen name for our profession, often rewarding me with a look of disdain.

From day one of my sales career as a beauty consultant at Bloomingdale's, I quickly learned that selling beauty products would be the easy part. It was the accompanying baggage – and I don't mean carry-on, that was jarring.

Many customers view the sales clerk behind the cosmetics counter as an airhead – somebody obsessed with her appearance, somebody who can't get a real job. Store associates outside the cosmetics department also shared this misconception. They were convinced that the gals in cosmetics did nothing all day except occasionally sell a lipstick. They labeled us "Cosmetic Queens."

Queens? Maybe. But to me we were, and will always be, a unique sales sisterhood unlike any other in retail.

We are the Rouge Hags.

Selling attracts a diverse pool of people from a wide range of economic, cultural and academic backgrounds. Cosmetics are theatre and fantasy. When many enter the beauty business, they are under the delusion that it will be glamorous, easy, and fun. When the Vaseline is removed from the lens, many are shocked to discover they actually have to work.

I equate selling with acting. You are on stage, and you are expected to give a winning performance. But on the cosmetics counter stage, you must make the customer feel that *she* is the star.

In the intertwined business of fashion, cosmetics and fragrances, competition is fierce and profit stakes are high. Stores have to compete with the Internet, discount and drugstores, infomercials, and home shopping. Even dermatologists and plastic surgeons have joined the profit parade with stocked shelves of skincare products and an array of *youth-enhancing* procedures. The fashion and cosmetics appetite of women will not be sated, which makes the industry recession-proof. I believe this is good. Rouge Hags find it uplifting to see folks well-groomed and taking pride in the way they present themselves.

Let's keep America beautiful!

BEAUTY

The human desire for beauty enhancement and self-decoration dates back to ancient times. Cosmetics have been used as long as there were people to use them. Primitive man used body and face painting for religious rituals, to attract the opposite sex, as well as to frighten enemies.

Ancient Egypt seriously embraced the culture of beauty. The signs of aging were a concern and various concoctions were formulated, including fats and oils to soften the skin. According to legend, Cleopatra bathed in ass milk and honey to soften her skin.

Egyptians focused on the eye. In addition to the cosmetics facet, the eye was considered the mirror of the soul and was a symbol of both good and evil.

In the 80s, during a trip to Asia, I was struck by the exquisite beauty of the Hong Kong female nightclub performers. Most of these women had eye surgery to westernize the shape of their eyes.

On a stop in Tokyo, I was impressed with the stylish Japanese women who seemed to be at the forefront of fashion. Their straight, black shiny hair and exotic eyes made for a striking picture. As always, the eyes have it.

In the United States, it was Greta Garbo who started the much-copied fashion of using black eyebrow pencil on the upper eyelid.

The image of beauty varies with regions and the passage of time. Lipstick, initially, was deemed shocking, however, it caught on fast and has become the most popular cosmetic. At one time, all cosmetics were held in contempt and considered to be immoral. They have emerged to become respectable and indispensable. Women have discovered the beauty-enhancing benefits and fun of makeup. Applying makeup is a calming ritual that also affords women a delightful sense of abandonment.

Today, the beauty business is a thriving multi-billion dollar industry. Cosmetic styles have evolved and the rage of the moment quickly becomes replaced by other styles. For example, the mole on a face was once accentuated with paint to draw attention to it.

Makeup was a factor in the John F. Kennedy versus Richard Nixon presidential debate in the sixties. The Kennedy camp realized that crafting a positive public image could create a major impact on the outcome of the election. Kennedy's youth, style and comfort level with the media, as well as his charisma and good looks were further enhanced with face makeup, allowing a picture of a healthy appearance. Nixon looked pale and frail due to a recent hospital stay for a knee infection. In addition, Nixon had a bout with the flu.

Though both were evenly matched, the general consensus declared JFK winner of the debate. Radio listeners called Nixon the winner, and television watchers declared JFK the winner.

The facelift, as a means of rejuvenation, was first used on the scars of soldiers' faces. The success of the procedure evolved into the practice of plastic surgery for beauty and youth enhancement. Plastic surgery is no longer only the realm of the rich and famous. The practice has become more acceptable and affordable, and technology has vastly improved.

Women, as well as men, also use plastic surgery to give them an edge with their careers.

Those who are determined to put their dreams into action will pursue the goal of changing their looks. A regular client, Mrs. Landis stopped at my cosmetics counter for body treatment. She matter –of- factly mentioned she would be going in for a partial face-lift. It was not to be her first. I'd buy a candy bar with less fanfare. I didn't think she needed a lift, but some women become addicted to the procedure once they've tasted the goods. There is always a part of the face or body that isn't perfect, and perfection is the goal.

Surgery addicts also bask in personal attention from medical professionals. Many plastic surgeons investigate the mental health of their patients before they commit them to the knife.

One of these cosmetics surgery junkies was the fifty-four year old author, Olivia Goldsmith, who wrote *The First Wives Club*, as well as many other books. In her search for acceptance and approval, she literally gave up her life. The heroines in her books often resorted to plastic surgery. Could she do less? It was thought to be the anesthesia, from which she never recovered.

ENTERING THE COSMETICS FIELD

In 1986, my husband Bernie and I moved to Westchester, New York. With only a high-school education and no marketable skills, I was jolted into the realization that I wasn't qualified for anything.

The timing was right for me to get a job. My kids were grown, and I was free of parental responsibility. But, I had not held a formal job for many years.

I spotted an ad for an Estee Lauder counter position at Bloomingdale's in White Plains. *I'll go for it – what could I lose?*

"What's the big hurry?" my sister Helen, who also lived in Westchester, wanted to know. She had anxiously awaited my move, looking forward to doing some serious shopping. In our language, that meant trying on everything in the store and then not buying anything, to be followed by lunch in an upscale restaurant.

Nonetheless, I made an appointment for the interview. I wasn't entirely inexperienced in cosmetics. In 1985, I was desperate for something to occupy my time, other than being a housewife. I was vague about the *something*.

I had met Ellen, a manager for Vanda Beauty Counselor skincare and cosmetics line, and she asked me to attend a regional meeting with her. The event took place in the general manager's home. Chairs were set up in rows, boxes containing products were piled high in the back of the room, and the front table displayed Vanda essentials.

The women at the meeting were warm and welcoming, as we learned about the products and saw makeup application demonstrations. Being a representative for a direct sales beauty line meant I could earn some pocket change and still be available to my kids.

Getting started was easy. I purchased my "beauty kit" a carrying case that resembled a diaper bag, which contained the essentials for skincare and makeup.

I was required to attend district sales meetings. Each meeting ended with an infantile pep rally, featuring the obnoxious song, "We Have Fun." Yes, a sappy song was meant to inspire us to produce mega sales!

WE HAVE FUN

Clear the way give us room

Watch our blossoms start to bloom

We are Vanda Beauty Counselors, a fact we don't assume

Hold the banners up high

Please salute when we go by

We are Vanda Beauty Counselors

And here's the reason why

When our gang's side by side, we have fun

We're a team one for all, all for one

My teenagers mocked the song and me by belting out the tune with a nasal twang.

Songs aside, for me, it was a new world to conquer. Would I be able to con women into buying the products?

I soon discovered that I had a talent for selling. I visited the customers' homes and set up shop, usually on the kitchen table. Although I'm not a coffee drinker, I always accepted a cup. I felt the klatch would ensure a fun and relaxed atmosphere for the customer.

On my first home visit, a teenager greeted me. Hands poised on her hips, a smirk on her mouth, she gave me an *I dare you* look. I could tell she was trouble, and trouble she was.

As I applied makeup to her mom's face, little "Miss Butinsky" corrected, second-guessed and poked fun at my efforts. I don't know who was more uncomfortable, the mother, or me. There was no sale.

My next appointment was to see one of the beautiful people at her beautiful home in a beautiful neighborhood. I psyched myself into making a large sale and made a huge effort to look as glamorous as the dream I was selling. I checked my makeup-case – yes, it was organized. The housemaid greeted me upon my arrival. I got as far as the foyer, when my potential client yelled down to me from the second floor. "This is not a good time to play with makeup," she called. My house looks like a cyclone hit it, and I will have to cancel."

Just like that! Another potential sale down the drain. (Her "messy" house looked better to me than my home looked at its neatest!)

In time, I did become skillful at prescribing treatments and applying makeup. I gained confidence, which was reflected in increased sales. At the end of each session, I asked the customer to supply me with the names of five friends, in exchange for a "gift" to be delivered with her order. You can bet that the gift wasn't a diamond, but rather samples and extras from my skincare and color stash. Before long, my sales were among the highest in my district, and the regional manager offered me a managerial position, which I accepted. My responsibilities included finding new recruits for the business as well as conducting sales meetings.

Disenchantment with my "promotion" set in quickly. Begging women to join the organization was difficult and distasteful. I held sales meetings in my home for a bunch of women, eighteen and older, who fantasized that a lot of money was made by doing a minimum amount of work. By unanimous consent, we named our group, "The Go-Getters." How is that for an imaginative title?

Often, I felt the need to apologize to my recruits for having to enforce Vanda rules, such as attaining sales quotas, being punctual for sales meetings, and participating in programs to test their knowledge and techniques. I apologized for the small amount of money they earned, for having to advise them not to bring their disruptive children to meetings, and for the commitment they needed to make to increase earnings.

To motivate the group, I used some of the methods employed at regional meetings. I created a friendly atmosphere. Refreshments were served, and every attendee received a small gift. However, my best efforts did not materialize into a successful operation. I felt exasperated that I failed to inspire these Vanda counselors to build a satisfying business for themselves.

Ultimately, I quit the farce that was my manager position. My group of beauty counselors was fortunate in one aspect. They were spared having to sing "We Have Fun."

BLOOMINGDALE'S

I stepped boldly into Bloomingdale's with only my Vanda cosmetics credit on my resume.

As I walked through the cosmetics landscape, I found myself in a sensory world of colors, scents, and cosmetics jargon. Calls of "Moisturizers" (one for the right cheek, one for the left) echoed throughout the department. Spritzers offered me fragrance cards of sweet, spicy, floral and woody scents. Promotions were at every turn – gifts, demonstrations, makeovers and invitations to try products.

"Can I offer you a free makeover?" asked a Lancôme makeup artist.

"No thank you, but would you please direct me to the personnel office?"

I felt a sense of anticipation, as well as apprehension, and for a brief moment questioned my desire to become a part of this fairyland.

After a successful first interview, with the cosmetics manager, I returned the following day for my next-level appointment with the operations manager, who was busy and suggested I browse the store and meet with her in an hour.

I tried on jackets in the sportswear department. Barbara, the saleslady, told me that I looked exceptionally well in a black blazer. I told her that if I clinched the cosmetics position, I would buy the jacket from her. You can never have too many black blazers.

I returned to the op-manager's office at the appointed time and was informed by her secretary that her previous meeting was still in progress. I waited an additional half hour. At that point, I asked the secretary where the meeting was taking place. She pointed to the room and added in a high-pitched voice, "Do not disrupt the meeting, that's the rule." I had to know the rules before I could break them, so I smiled at her, knocked on the door and shoehorned my way in. The attendees, sitting in a circle, looked dumfounded as I plopped myself in the center and addressed the op-manager to remind her of our appointment an hour-and-a half ago. The person who seemed to be in charge apologized to me and released the op-manager.

Emboldened by my venture in the conference room, I was relaxed, confident, and performed well during the interview. I felt that it wouldn't matter anyway, since the young humorless op-manager most likely wouldn't hire me. To my surprise, she signed me up. But I had the feeling that she would deposit the conference room incident in her memory bank for future withdrawal. Yes, she would make me pay for my audacity.

I was also interviewed by the Estee Lauder account executive. This was a piece of cake, and she readily approved me for the vacant position. The gate swung open, and I entered the Bloomingdale's cosmetics community.

In spite of the early craziness, Bloomies became my playground, and I soon became a true Cosmetics Queen.

ESTEE LAUDER

On my first day at the Estee Lauder counter, Maryann, the young and dumb counter manager, greeted me with a scowl. "You look like a banker in your gray blazer and white blouse."

What difference did it make that I reported to work in a tailored outfit, I wondered. I was required to wear the frumpy green Estee Lauder uniform at the counter, so I would be changing anyway.

Maryann also said, "Where did you learn to apply makeup? You look bland."

Doris, another co-worker instantly perceived me as a threat, since we were both "mature women," and the other associates were sales children whom she could manipulate. She "welcomed" me by saying, "I don't know why they put you here – we have enough people as it is." The rest of the crew either ignored me or were reluctant to answer my questions concerning policies and products.

Clearly, I needed to toughen up and make some personality adjustments to fit in.

I learned that Estee Lauder, founder of the company, which bears her name, began by selling her uncle's skincare formulations to friends and beauty shops. The company grew into one of the largest cosmetics conglomerates in the world, with holdings like Mac, Clinique, Origins, Prescriptives, Aveda, Bobby Brown, Stila, and Tommy Hilfiger. This information helped me to appreciate the scope of the cosmetics line I worked for.

After a week with Lauder, Maryann accompanied me to the stock room and directed me to unpack and shelve the contents of the huge amount of boxes in the dark and musty room.

Cleansers and toners for dry skin, extra dry skin, oily skin, sensitive skin, and combination skincare came in many sizes and price categories. Moisturizers formulated for all skin types were in liquid or cream forms – again in various size sets and price ranges. There were specialty skin preparations such as concealers, daytime treatments, treatments for nighttime, and mature skin treatments. Whatever the specialty, Lauder had it.

The sets were attractively packaged in multiples and were often used for promotions or sales incentives. The color foundations were especially challenging to sort because there were so many formulas. Eye treatments and makeup, body treatments, fragrances, bonuses and gift beauty aids needed to be unpacked. Whew! I was decimated. Whatever aptitude needed to deal with the confusing hodgepodge that confronted me, I lacked.

At the end of the day, I was ready to collapse. Maryann reprimanded me since I finished only half the task at hand. When I stammered that I was unfamiliar with the overwhelming amount of products, she retorted, "You know how to read English, don't you?"

Closing the cash register at the end of the day was another bewildering task. I felt too squeamish to ask for help from my associates, because register training was part of my indoctrination. Closings were rotated among the associates, but I was told by Maryann to close on consecutive days until "You get it right." Was I being punished for something?

Doris was also an issue for me. In her sixties, she had a pretty face, matronly figure, and a slow gait. Her hair was gray – so was mine, although that was a secret between the bottle and me. Once, and only once, I asked

Doris for help – to point out the drawer for a specific blush. I was serving a customer. She flashed a blank look and walked away.

Doris was territorial and glued herself to one corner, which was like a busy intersection, with traffic from all directions. This gave her a tremendous advantage to approach customers. I was tempted to stand in her spot while she serviced customers, but quickly abandoned that idea. I knew enough not to pile additional baggage onto my existing difficulties.

Soon after my arrival at Lauder, I witnessed one example of how sales are shamelessly pursued. The production number began when Barbara, a regular customer showed up again with Sethy, her 2-year-old son. The sales associates were aware of Barbara's addiction as a cosmetics junkie and showed no mercy. Barb made the rounds, visiting her favorite cosmetics counters, which seemed to be all of them.

She did an outstanding job of spoiling her son. He screamed, kicked and took joy in knocking over anything that attracted him. The associates approached Sethy to hug him, and he rewarded them with kicks. He also didn't hesitate to spit at them when they tried to kiss him. Barb did not reprimand him; rather the employees who competed with each other for her business cheered Sethy on. They had fine-tuned their act. Sales at any cost.

Doris practically went into convulsions trying to outdo her associates in indulging Barb and Sethy. Her usual low and slow voice morphed into nervous speed.

"Hi, Barbara, and you too, young man." Most likely, she forgot his name. "I'm delighted to see you. I can't wait to show you our new colors."

I was an amused observer of these maneuvers. I felt that I could improve on my co-workers' desperate attempts. I would seduce Sethy with small fun goodies and candy. In addition I would load Barb with notable cosmetics gifts from my stash.

After a week with Bloomingdale's, two Lauder representatives paid an unexpected visit to test my knowledge of the Lauder products. They asked several pages of questions while I was at the counter, as customers watched. I felt embarrassed and humiliated since I could not answer many questions. To the representatives' credit, no negative comments came forth. However, they promised me another visit in a week, explaining that the procedure was routine for newcomers. I had not yet attended the official Estee Lauder "school" for thorough training.

Sometime after starting with Lauder, I found myself alone in the employee lunchroom with Doris. We had not spoken to each other for quite some time. I wanted to smile at her to break the ice, but my Novocain lipstick inhibited that. It was Doris who spoke up and she apologized for having been unfair to me! She disclosed her imminent retirement from Bloomingdale's within a month.

Doris confessed she had wanted to keep control of the counter and felt my menacing presence. She realized her behavior towards me was unjustified and mean spirited. Now in retrospect, she felt ashamed and wanted to leave of good accord.

I applaud Doris's honesty and sincerity and felt extremely gratified. My former ill will was replaced by kind feelings towards her, and I wished her luck on her retirement.

Ultimately, but not surprisingly, Maryann reported me to the op-manager for being slow, uncooperative and *not fitting in*. Now the op-manager had her chance to release her pent up hostility over the meeting incident. Gleefully, she told me that I had one week to straighten out. Clearly, the issue was not about selling. That day, I lost my "sales virginity." It was now a different ball game. No more Ms. Nice Guy. I'd show them I could be tough, too!

In spite of my bold resolve, I agonized that maybe I was not predisposed to work for a large, prestigious upscale department store. This was a different orbit from selling coffee klatch Vanda. This was the real world: cash registers, procedures, customers, co-workers, managers, and politics. Maybe I just couldn't cut it.

Nancy, the cosmetics department manager, saw me differently. She confided that she had been watching me and felt I could outsell all of the Lauder ladies. My sales were healthy in spite of the troublesome conditions. Nancy proposed a position with Stendhal, an elegant, pricey French cosmetics line. It paid a high commission since it was a small line and produced low volume sales. Nancy gave me a good sales pitch and I accepted her offer. The Lauder regional manager, who was instrumental in hiring me, urged me to stay with Lauder since she was happy with my performance. She gave my low morale a boost, but I had already made up my mind to leave Lauder.

Besides, I didn't like those horrid green uniforms.

STENDHAL AND BIOTHERM

Estee Lauder and its accompanying obstacles were my training wheels, not only for the cosmetics department, but also for the school of life.

Lauder was an easy sell. One could "cashier" the line and still end up with decent sales. To cashier means to fill the customer's request, without putting forth much effort to increase the sale. Without the volume mega lines enjoyed, Stendhal had to be *worked*.

I ran the counter by myself. Stendhal encouraged me to be creative and to plan promotions and facials on my own. This was a far cry from the restrictive and hostile atmosphere at Lauder.

My enthusiasm was transparent. When new stock arrived, I felt like a child opening birthday presents. My peers across the aisle good-naturedly sneered as they observed my excitement.

Fiercely, I wanted to succeed with my new line. The previous Stendhal associate allowed the line to flounder. I had to prove that I could do better. I learned fast about the inducements to foster a sale. The savvy sales associate doesn't ask, "What size?" She simply reaches for the large *economy* size.

I now used Stendhal products, and the positive change in my skin's appearance became noticeable. I was seduced by the quality of the treatments, the riot of colors, as well as the sophisticated packaging. Treatments were packaged in imitation tortoise shell, and colors were cased in slick black containers.

Discriminating customers appreciated the high quality of the French treatments and were attracted to the vivid Stendhal color palette. They didn't mind parting with their lucre to take home the booty.

Four small cosmetics lines resided on my new bay, a four-sided counter. In spite of my short stint with Lauder, I was still considered the newbie. One person was assigned to each line, and we were all counter managers.

A customer made a purchase for $700 on my second day with Stendhal. This was considered a huge sale for the small line and didn't happen frequently. The customer knew exactly what she wanted, so I didn't have to *sell* her. The transaction wasn't lost on my bay-mates and nearby associates. I didn't win the Miss Congeniality award that day.

That same week, a customer bought a substantial amount of skincare products from me. Brenda, the counter manager for Germaine Monteil on my bay, who was obsessed with her two-year nasty divorce litigation, strutted over and called me a greedy bastard. She insisted I stole her customer, announcing, "That woman always buys from me." I explained to Brenda that the woman approached me, and of course I tried to make a sale. This bone of contention lodged between us for the remainder of my stay at that bay. In another life, I most likely would have been quite fond of Brenda.

At Stendhal training class, the hands-on lessons were extremely helpful, and the abundance of products I took home didn't hurt either. Stendhal was boot camp on the art of selling, which served me well throughout my sales career.

Stendhal required a $40 deposit to participate in their treatment and makeover events, which took place in the facial room adjacent to the upstairs beauty parlor. Full attendance was assured because of the infrequency of the event (every three or four months) and the loyalty of Stendhal customers. A freelancer helped me set up the room. Posters, product testers, Perrier water and other refreshments were set up. The scent of fresh cut flowers and soft music permeated the spa. This class act produced brisk sales from the royally treated customers.

After two months with Stendhal, I was offered an additional line – Biotherm, another French company. This meant more selling options and the opportunity for additional income. Biotherm had more of a general clientele. The ingredients of the skincare products were of the highest quality. The packaging was plain and user-friendly.

Both companies paid me identical commissions, and though I would have earned more from high-priced Stendhal, I directed the customers toward the most appropriate product, even if it was less expensive Biotherm. My goal was to build trust and have the customer return.

For me, the job didn't end at the store. I waived my breakfast ritual reading the newspaper to immerse myself in study of Stendhal and Biotherm products. The information I absorbed resulted in a heightened comfort level at the counter.

A Lauder big spender stopped at my counter. She remembered me from the Lauder bay, although she had not purchased from me. I gave her my well-rehearsed sales pitch, at the same time pressing samples into her hand.

Maryann, my previous Lauder counter manager, slinked over and yelled a big "Hi, how are you?" to the customer.

Both hands on my hips, I walked over to Maryann, asking, "Is there anything I can do for you and if not, get the hell out of here before I call the manager."

You can't make an omelet without cracking an egg. After my confrontation, I never had to crack an egg over Maryann again.

Working Stendhal and Biotherm left me feeling overwhelmed and overworked. However, the boost in pay soothed my psyche. After a year, both lines were removed from all Bloomingdale's stores, as well as all department stores. It was a sad turn of events for me. Both lines did exceptionally well in my store, and I didn't hesitate to brag about it.

SALES

Whether window-shopping, or making a purchase, the buying experience gives me a lift. Research indicates that shopping releases chemicals in the brain that make a person feel uplifted. But I knew that all along.

Sales was king in the department store, and a salesperson's measuring stick. Competition, among sales associates could be fierce, and fostered aggressive and sometimes ugly behavior. It was not uncommon for associates to scream at each other on the sales floor. This unprofessional behavior was embarrassing to whoever was within earshot. These outbursts were often the result of "stealing customers" – which may have been a perception. Some gals felt that saying "Good morning" or "Hello" to a customer conferred ownership. Or, they may have serviced the customer at a previous visit and put a claim on her.

I stopped at the near-by stock room to get an item requested by my customer. She was poised to sign up for a Stendhal facial. Upon returning just seconds later, Brenda was in the process of signing her up for one of her events. There was no $40 pre-pay as with Stendhal. I directed dagger looks at both, and left it at that.

It's moments like this, when I'm nauseated to be a part of a culture that dehumanizes for the sake of profit.

Then there was "Barracuda Bay." It seemed every store was infested with at least one of these sites: a bay inhabited by vigorously aggressive, devious, calculating and dishonest Rouge Hags.

Essentially, the problem was inherent in the structure. Let's say, there were three associates working for the same cosmetics line. All three gals vied for the same customer. If customer attendance was low and the cosmetics line was not one of the fast-moving mega companies, such as Lancôme, Clinique or Estee Lauder, the situation became acute. Tensions mounted as the day progressed and the realization set in that you would not make your sales goal, or even come close. When the precious commodity, the customer, appeared, the three associates practically ran her down. Taking turns was an option, but didn't always work.

My advice to the winner of the sale, especially a BIG SALE, is don't open a bottle of champagne yet. The inevitable sticker shock and dreaded big return always loomed.

Many men have a difficult time with returns. My husband, Bernie, won the chicken award for that. He either kept his "mistake" or he started offering me five dollars to do his dirty work. "I don't come that cheap," I would tell him. Then he upped the ante, and I headed for the store.

CLARINS

Clarins was unhappy with its counter manager at my store and wanted a replacement. This occurred at the time Stendhal and Biotherm were pulled out of Bloomies. Talk about timing! Nancy asked me to interview for Clarins, yet another French line. French treatments and colors were considered the gold standard in the cosmetics world.

I was ready! By then, I was a *pro*.

Very tall, dark and gorgeous, Eric Horowitz, son of the president of Clarins U.S.A., interviewed me. Unfortunately, the blood vessels in one eye burst the day of the interview, and my eye was bathed in tomato red. I reasoned that at least the eye matched the red Clarins uniform!

Eric, the champion nitpicker, as I later discovered, scrutinized me. So I put him out of his misery and archly explained that my eye was not infectious and that I had merely walked into my husband's fist. I don't think he was amused.

But Nancy had put in a good word for me. The interview was short, and Eric asked, "When can you start?"

Periodically, Eric along with his handsome and sophisticated father, Mr. Horowitz, who was president, paid a visit to my Bloomingdale's.

When father and son arrived at the store, they always greeted me with a kiss on the cheek. It was fun to banter and joke with them, as well as to discuss business. What was even more fun was that all the cosmetics gals' green eyes were fixated on my counter.

Eric ran his finger over a counter lampshade checking for dust. Since he didn't catch me on this one, he proceeded to another lampshade to repeat the finger test.

"What are you – my mother-in law?" I asked him. Eric's dad laughed loud and hard, delighted whenever I berated his son.

Laura, a strikingly attractive, tall Clinique associate, pleaded with me to get her a date with Eric. I refused – procurer was not a part of my job description. She badgered me until she wore me down. The next time I saw Eric, I flat out asked him. He was the total gentleman, requesting I thank Laura and tell her he was flattered, but he doesn't mix business with pleasure.

Laura's response was, "Forget the business, I really want him only for pleasure."

The women loved to pursue Eric, sometimes quite aggressively, but in spite of his commanding presence, he was somewhat shy and naïve about his charm, good looks and appeal, not to mention his high ranking at Clarins. He is now married and has a family. He also became president of Clarins U.S.A.

I once asked Eric, as did most Clarins employees, "Will Clarins ever offer a "free gift?" His reply, "We give them the gift of knowledge." Yeah? Try putting that in your shopping bag! He reminded me that Clarins generously gives free samples and complimentary facials, but that the brand's emphasis is not so much on marketing, as it is on serving the customer.

It must work, since nationally, business continued to increase at a brisk pace.

Clarins and Lancôme shared a bay. I loved working with the Lancôme gals. They were young and savvy, and did a decent job selling in spite of the fact that boys and clothes were their prime interests. Being the senior on the bay, I was elected advisor to the lovelorn. Since they switched boyfriends weekly, I was kept busy.

The Lancôme/Clarins bay faced the escalators, and was squarely situated in a high-traffic zone, making the location desirable. Nevertheless, Clarins coveted the location at the mall entrance to the cosmetics department. The entrance was considered to be the prime parcel for visibility, accessibility and robust traffic. Clarins put in a request for this exclusive property.

Clarins had a juicy past with Bloomies, once pulling out the entire chain over a mysterious dispute. Since returning to Bloomies, Clarins enjoyed considerable clout within the store, so naturally, we won the prime real estate.

In the cosmetics world, every victory launched a scene from the loser, and the counter manager for the flashy line we ousted from the front bay took the eviction personally, throwing a tantrum as they moved her out.

"My line is better known and more important than Clarins. You won't do any business here because the customers will all ask for me and my line."

The fragrance department was opposite the new Clarins location, a benefit as it created additional traffic. Andrew, a fragrance spritzer, proved to be a good neighbor. I cringed at his silly phrases, like when he asked, "Have you had lunchy-poo yet?" The sad part was I soon found myself using the phrase.

Believe me, my husband/kids weren't so keen on me serving them lunchy-poo!

Arlene

One of the occupants on the new Clarins bay was Elizabeth Arden. The other, Adrian Arpel. The Arpel girls were fun and terrific, and we had a great relationship. They gave me their night cream testers to shine and soften my leather boots. Their zany acts kept business tensions in proper perspective.

Arden was another story. Arlene, counter manager for Arden, was attractive, well-groomed and stylishly dressed, as well as being a dedicated and hard-working representative for her line. Arlene was past the usual retirement age, and when asked by co-workers when would she relinquish her job, she answered with a straight face, "I can't retire. My customers need me and I can't disappoint them."

My arrival on the bay was bad news for Arlene. She felt threatened by Clarins and by me. Immediately, she asked me to move our color display unit because she deemed it too high for her customers to see her. But, my account executive and I had set up the counter to make it attractive, inviting and functional. I told Arlene the display unit would remain where it was.

One day, while dusting my showcase, I placed some makeup brushes on *her* counter-space. A serious mistake! Without saying a word, she picked up the brushes and plopped them on my counter.

My brother-in-law and his wife paid a surprise visit to the store and observed the makeup brush affair from afar. He came to the counter and quietly gave me a tip: "Screw her in the liver."

Although I liked my brother-in-law's candid advice, I couldn't literally act on it. But ignore her I could.

Ms. Wiggins

Ms. Wiggins, our New York Clarins trainer, was a consummate professional, which she believed required her to exhibit nasty and rigid behavior. Periodically, she appeared at Bloomingdale's presiding over a breakfast, to introduce new Clarins products and review the collection of existing beauty aids.

All cosmetics department employees were invited to the breakfasts, since a sale could result when a customer asked for a Clarins product, though not at a Clarins counter.

Ms Wiggins was a contradiction. Her British accent, tall blond good looks and cheerfulness were seductive. She was fastidiously groomed, fashionably dressed and oh, so poised, bordering on too much formality. She also had a nervous laugh, almost a schoolgirl giggle, which she used inappropriately. After Breakfast, she always asked, "Have you had sufficient?"

The cosmetics department employees were charmed and beguiled by her. However, the Clarins employees, who attended her schools and were more familiar with Ms. Wiggins's tactics, took a different view. We recognized the flip side to all that charm and saccharin.

At the New York City training sessions held in a hotel, attended by surrounding area Clarins employees, she ruled with a serious, no-nonsense attitude and expected the same from us. She was also sarcastic and snippy. Most of us were uncomfortable in her presence.

Once while describing skin functions, she said, "Did you know that the top layer of the skin is called the *horny layer?*" She then laughed convulsively.

Her school sessions ended at 5 o'clock and not a minute sooner. Her mean side surfaced one day when an associate asked to leave ten minutes early. Her physically handicapped husband planned to pick her up by car and wanted to avoid the rush of everyone leaving at the same time. Ms. Wiggins would not allow this modest request.

During that session, we had makeup application practice. Each lady had a partner, and the game plan was to practice on each other. The face was to be cleaned; treatments and color were to follow. I needed to avoid this procedure. "Ms. Wiggins, I'd like to be excused from having my partner practice on my face, however, I'd be happy to do her face." Before I could finish my request, she said, "Absolutely not."

"Ms. Wiggins," I protested politely, "my skin is extremely sensitive and I already did the cleansing and color ritual at home. If I have to repeat this procedure, I'd have a skin flare-up."

"You are here to participate, and if you can't do that, then you have no business being in this business."

I sweetly said, "Thank you," and walked away.

I had sufficient.

I suspected that she reported this drama to Eric.

Ms. Wiggins was ultimately dismissed from her lofty job because of security reasons. Something about padding her expense account?

Later I learned that I suffered from the skin condition called rosacea. The telltale signs are reddened skin, which can be triggered by food, temperature extremes, stress, and some facial products. President Bill Clinton also has the condition, a fact that, illogically, made me feel better.

No need to feel sorry for me because of my rosacea. I milked it wherever I could. My dermatologist wrote a note explaining I could not tolerate weather extremes, and I reasoned with the personnel department that it wouldn't make sense to have a skincare/cosmetics "expert" with a face breakout. I was assigned a parking space close to the employee's entrance.

Soon after my association with Clarins, the skincare/cosmetics line Origins entered the market at Bloomingdale's. The fact that Origins is under the Estee Lauder umbrella, and also that Origins claimed to use plants in its products (as did Clarins), raised a red flag for me. I regarded the Origins presence a menace, and justifiably so.

Origins proved to be innovative with a truly high quality line and clever marketing maneuvers. During the holiday season, they outdid themselves with smart pricing and packaging, and business was outstanding.

How I suffered!

FREE GIFTS

The mega lines, Estee Lauder, Clinique, Lancôme, Christian Dior, and copycats put much emphasis and reliance on "Free Gift." A gift is a gift – why call it free?

The foreplay began at a rally, which took place either at a hotel or in the store. This was followed by "presale." Walk-up customers, as well as those from existing files, were informed of the event. Customers didn't need to be concerned about a gift shortage, since at least a two-week supply was available for the weekly gift promotion, which was then extended.

Employees were rewarded with merchandise and other incentives for high pre-sales figures. The mega lines advertised their promotions in local newspapers, radio and T.V. On the premiere "Gift" day, employees were required to start two hours before the store opened to be prepared for the customers.

The "Free Gift" event is ingrained in the cosmetics culture, both for the customers and cosmetics lines. Many customers saved up their purchases and waited for the "Gift" event, which occurred several times annually.

Showtime – let the games begin.

The customers couldn't wait to get their hands on something free. It's a one-size fits all, and even though many items were useless, it hardly mattered. Some lines had even begun offering options for skin and color products to personalize the give-away.

The customer was obliged to spend $30 or more, to qualify for the "Gift," but only one was allowed per customer. The savvy salesperson found ways to work around this restriction and gave the customers two or more gifts for their *friends* or *daughters,* if the size of the purchase justified it.

The "Gifts" consisted of trial or sample size assortments of skincare and makeup. Sometimes manicure sets, makeup brushes, mirrors and other related items were packaged inside makeup purses. Additional gifts were offered, such as tote bags or travel items, if the customer's expenditure warranted it.

Prior to my entry into the cosmetics field, I also yielded to the "Gift" phenomenon. I mused these "Gifts" would be great playthings for little girls, who could practice makeup skills on their dolls, and if mommies permitted, on themselves.

Employees worked long hours and were under pressure to attain high sales, which at times prompted both the sales associates and customers to display bizarre behavior. My proximity to Clinique afforded me a perfect observation point.

A Clinique associate overheard a customer ask for an extra gift. "You were here yesterday, and I gave you an extra gift for your mother," she shrieked to the customer and to the person servicing the "greedy" one. "Don't give her an extra gift."

"It's none of your business!" The customer shrieked back. "I'm a good customer, and if you don't shut your fat mouth, I'll call the manager."

The cosmetics lines not in "Gift" at the time tended to lose some sales, because even loyal customers will cross over for a chance at the "Gift." Although with the huge volume of customers generated by the event, some did find their way to other cosmetics counters.

A little powder, a little paint
makes a gal what she ain't

MAKEUP ARTISTS

For those not willing to go under the knife, makeup is their path to a new look.

Makeup artists feel empowered when brandishing their assorted makeup brushes. National Makeup Artists are at the top of their profession in the glamour industry, commanded high pay, and were sought after by the luminaries. One can achieve designation as a National Makeup Artist. The locals employed by department stores are not in this category, but often acted "as if."

Some may have started their position only the previous day and many had no experience in applying color. This fact didn't stop the overnight makeup mavens from wielding their brushes. Some of the results of their labor were horrific. Sadly, many customers didn't get it. As long as lots of color was applied, they felt they got their money's worth.

The National Makeup Artist was another sales inducement in the cosmetics department. Customers were eager to sign up for the promise of transformation at the hands of the best. Many were men. Are they more talented, more creative, better qualified, and better looking than the local makeup artists? Do they have a foreign accent? Many women find the accent irresistible. I found that both local and National Makeup Artists were equally adept at performing their job.

The customers, staff and associates fell for the hype "flown in". The National Makeup Artists were given star treatment from the store and vendors.

The red carpet was literally rolled out – it led to the makeup throne. Freelance makeup artists prepared the face with cleansers, moisturizers, and eye cream. Then the Nationals applied color. Thus, more customers were served, and there was more efficient use of the "flown-in" deity.

The ambience and excitement created contributed to the success of the event. The flower arrangements were bigger and more exotic, the refreshments more elaborate, and the pampering more excessive, creating a party atmosphere. No less important, was the flying hero snob appeal. Also, the pre-pay, requirement added weight to the occasion.

Unfortunately, the hygienic aspects of makeovers were often deplorable. Much double-dipping occurred. Many cosmetics lines cleansed their brushes with alcohol or washed them in the store bathroom sinks. Having witnessed the sanitizing attempts, I was unconvinced of the thoroughness and effectiveness of the procedure. It's a crapshoot. In this age of disease proliferation, it is astonishing that this careless practice was permitted.

I'd like to emphasize that not *all* cosmetics lines adhered to this unhealthy disregard for the customers' safety and well-being.

It's a scandal that could easily be remedied by supplying germ-free individually wrapped colors, applicators, and other makeup related items. But that would cost money.

I am knocking aspects of a business that has afforded me much pleasure, satisfaction and a generous income, but I feel strongly that some negative elements of that business should not be overlooked.

CO-WORKERS

Willem de Kooning, the Dutch artist, said, "Nothing is original –it's all alphabet soup – you pick a letter." I'm not sure that I agree.

Those invested in the arts, will often act outrageously in their quest for originality and shock. The eccentric co-workers I encountered, had no agenda to achieve fame by hawking cosmetics in a department store, but most are one-of-a-kind originals.

Most sales persons want to be productive, to be kept busy, and to achieve job satisfaction as well as scratching out a living. These components have to be present to feel fulfilled at the end of the day. Some associates' agendas are directed towards having fun, discussing their manicures, tattoos, clothes, and their boyfriends. For them, the big sale or any sale is a distraction and an abstraction. The associates that I worked with were a smorgasbord. Some were talented and serious salespeople, some were indifferent, and some displayed bizarre behavior, but most were likeable and charming just the same.

The Rouge Hags created plenty of drama in the cosmetics department. But even without these powerful personalities, the beauty business was naturally colorful.

The Sophia Debacle

After I had been with Clarins a few months, a new thirty-something associate named Sophia was hired, and I was taken in by her engaging personality. When my husband stopped by one day and met Sophia, he warned me not to trust her. "She will cause you grief," Bernie said. "She has shifty eyes." Nonsense, I thought. She has beautiful blue eyes and strikingly good looks.

Although Sophia had facial certification, she was clueless about selling. "This is the day cream, you use it in the daytime – this is the night cream, you use it in the night time," she recited. Pathetic! I felt smug since I knew so much more about the cosmetics business. Yet I was eager to teach her the ropes and share the benefit of my experience, since we would equally profit. As counter manager, I would get an override, a percentage of everything she sold. Also, a productive and smoothly running counter would reflect favorably on both of us.

Sophia was a fast learner and wasted no time reaching her potential. While there was nothing wrong with her goals, her methods of achieving them were ruthless. She hid products that were in short supply to have the items available for *her* sales. She used the same ploy with samples. Also, she put false names in the facial appointment book in order to save space for *her* customers, at the same time limiting my own bookings.

Often Sophia screeched over my shoulder "Can I help you?" After I had already acknowledged a customer. She did some fancy bootlicking and invited some of the management staff to her home. They all declined because it had a whiff of something unethical. After several weeks with Sophia, I no longer looked forward to coming to work.

I considered myself to be an aggressive sales person. I vigorously pursued and worked the customers to get as many sales as I could. However I knew when to step aside and give my co-workers the same opportunity.

One morning, Sophia practically tackled a customer and told her she'd like to show her the Clarins line. "I'm sorry, but I'm looking for Marlit. My daughter wants her to help me," said the customer. She explained that her daughter, a regular customer of mine, was hospitalized and sent her mother to pick up her usual supply of skincare and color products, which were always a sizable amount. In addition, the daughter wanted me to select body products for her hospital stay. Before leaving, the mother even signed up for an upcoming facial. Had she not been insistent on working with me, Sophia would have usurped a substantial commission.

I did not take Sophia's assaults lying down. We both agreed that management intervention was necessary. I confess I felt threatened by Sophia's increasing sales, which seemed to be furthered by her underhanded methods. I enumerated her tactics to management and also pointed out that customers sensed the discord at the counter. Sophia felt that I should have been more supportive and encouraging of her efforts, after all, that's what a counter manager was supposed do. She also said that I withheld information.

The rhetoric swung back and forth; an appalling display of deficient maturity on both our parts. Management abruptly stopped the self-righteous orgy. They told us that we were both valuable and viable salespersons and we should try harder to get along.

It was difficult to keep working together since we were miserable in each other's presence. Bernie's prophecy was fulfilled. As often happens, fate stepped in. Soon after the management meeting, Sophia applied for and got a position at another cosmetics counter. The aftershock of the Sophia debacle resulted in the loss of my enthusiasm for imparting my experience and knowledge to newcomers.

Sweetpea and Peewee

That's what I called the two new Clinique associates. They were in their twenties, full of life and mischief, and so cute. Don't ask me their hair color, since it was never the same for more than a week.

I complimented Sweetpea on her color of the week – eggplant. I took a strand of her hair and placed it close to my face. As we scrutinized the look in the mirror, we concluded the color was good for my skin tone. The two young friends urged, goaded, pleaded, and threatened me to *do* it. I was bored with my bottled brown hair color anyway, and thought, why not?

After I had completed the job, I invited my husband to the bathroom. He gasped.

"You look like a floozy," he exclaimed. "When we're in public just walk ahead of me."

I sported my new "do" at the workplace and received many comments; some were even complimentary. Sweetpea and Peewee were thrilled and loved, loved, loved not only the hair color, but also the fact that I didn't chicken out. I was accepted in their tight inner sanctum.

They showered me with Clinique samples, confided their love lives, and shared off-color jokes. They even directed customers to me.

Get Me a Pill!

Debbie, a new Clarins addition, discovered vegetarianism at the age of nineteen and had been a devout believer and practitioner for three years. Her mission was to convert all who came in contact with her to her meat-free religion, as well as subject the employees to her food tirades. She asked us what we had or will have for breakfast, lunch and dinner and snickered when the answers didn't measure up to her standards. Not everyone wanted a sermon with their moisturizer.

Debbie reminded me of a quote I love from celebrity chef Anthony Bourdain: "Vegetarians are the enemy of everything good and decent in the human spirit."

Debbie's eyes were the bluest blue and the white of her eyes were the whitest white, enhancing her pretty face. She attributed the clarity and vivid colors of her eyes to her diet.

Despite her preaching, we soon discovered we shared a passion: a middle-eastern dish called mujadara. Because of our mutual love affair with healthy mujadara, Debbie began to bypass customers and steered them to me. She reasoned she'd be leaving soon and didn't need the sales.

Debbie's food issues weren't the only annoyances the associates had to endure. Her upcoming wedding became an even greater obsession. It was to be a huge affair with 300 guests. The customers and associates were bombarded with detailed descriptions: the bridal gown and bridesmaid's dresses, shoes, jewelry, headpieces, a fragrance for her, and a different fragrance for the bridesmaids. The menu would be geared for "unhealthy food people" although vegetarian fare would also be offered.

She seemed to be registered in every nationwide store. With agonizing monotone, she droned on about her wish list at each store; dish patterns, silverware, cooking utensils, broiler, toaster, George Foreman grill, sandwich maker, on and on. She doubted her future in-laws would be as generous with gifts as her parents. I received a bridal shower gift subpoena in the mail.

She declared she'd be "out of here" after the wedding, which was two months away. We waited for a miracle to hasten her departure. Someone most likely prayed non-stop, because the miracle came to pass.

Our blushing vegetarian bride arrived one morning in a spastic state. Tearfully she blubbered the wedding was off, and she was quitting her job.

Her fiancé had left and run off with a meat eater.

More from the Rouge Gallery

Cindy, the Shiseido counter manager, was out to lunch, and a customer asked for my help. Cindy returned from her lunch break and spotted me in the process of ringing a sale at her counter. Glaring at me, she blatantly pushed the register tabs to stop and void the transaction. "That's *my* customer," she said. I had followed proper procedure.

Cindy also kept herself busy minding everyone else's business. By manipulating the cash registers at Bloomingdale's, current sales figures for all cosmetics and fragrance counters could be obtained. Associates like Cindy wanted to compare their own sales with those of the competition and found the practice irresistible. It was self-inflicted punishment, since invariably, someone else's sales figures were higher.

＊＊＊＊

Another counter girl, Lilly had a meltdown as she spoke to her husband on the phone. He had been in a traffic accident. Lilly was out of control as she cried and screamed and declared she would immediately leave the store to be with her husband.

Oops – she spotted a potential sale at *another counter*. Quickly hanging up on her poor hubby, she went for it. A look of triumph appeared on her face after she got the sale.

CLARINS SCHOOLS

Clarins conducted one-day training classes for the skin care specialists twice yearly. New products were introduced, existing products reviewed, and makeup application skills honed and updated. The account executives and store cosmetics manager usually attended these schools. The skin care specialists were aware they were being evaluated for performance and participation. The presence of managers created uneasiness and stifled spontaneity.

Clarins heir apparent, Eric Horowitz, was scheduled to appear at one particular school, and it was difficult for me to get a decent night's sleep because of the anticipated tension. I was wound tight, when Eric asked how I was, and mentioned my sleep deprivation. As soon as those words escaped my lips, I wanted to kick myself with cleated shoes. The unwritten rule is to project a positive and upbeat attitude.

At the start of the session, Eric gave his presentation. He was an effective, entertaining speaker, and his good looks and charm didn't hurt!

During Eric's talk, he used the analogy of airplane pilots to describe the skincare specialists' responsibilities. He wanted to drive home that excellence is expected at all times and excuses are not acceptable. Airline passengers whose lives are in the pilots' hands demand and are entitled to top performance. Clients, he said, need the same level of commitment from us.

"How do you think the airplane passengers would react to an announcement by the pilot that he was feeling rather tired since he had a poor night's sleep?" Eric didn't look at me when he posed that question. He didn't have to.

SKIN CARE CENTER

The Clarins Skin Care Center is an institution. Each *Instructrice De Beaute* received thorough and ongoing training to ensure they were highly qualified and capable.

Our approach was to offer the client a complimentary facial. "Sit them in the chair and treat them," one account executive instructed. At the end of the facial day, the instructrice, who was accountable for a facial sales quota, had to report the sales generated to her account executive.

Who doesn't like a free lunch? I learned fast that just offering a complimentary facial, for the most part, produced little, if any sales. I was direct and made it clear to the client that the facial was indeed complimentary, however, it's done only with a purchase. It worked. The co-workers who couldn't handle the reality of straight talk often ended up disappointed.

The facial events were educational, relaxing, and fun for clients. The events also produced tension for skin care specialists, who vied for sales. Add to that the products and paraphernalia mess behind the counter. However, at the end of the day, they were profitable.

While the majority of facial clients were female, a few courageous men occupied the chair. They did not feel their masculinity threatened; rather they took skin care seriously and were a pleasure to work with. The husband and wife teams were also great fun and competed for the "good stuff" they purchased, resulting in substantial sales.

One of the regulars at the Skin Care Center was

a male specimen in his forties. He synchronized his moans and groans with each massage stroke, matching each stroke with different noise levels. He kept both hands underneath the white cloth draped over him. One could only speculate. Much as the instructrice dreaded the pervert, she didn't discourage his visits, since he consistently flaunted his wad of bills and plunked down big bucks.

Two men from the homeless fringe of society had discovered a good thing. They came in for facials to get out of the cold, as well as for pampering and relaxation, not to mention a free face wash. They had no phones and addresses, but never failed to show up for their appointments. The instructrice was kind-hearted enough to indulge them. She ignored the fact they were dirty and toothless. At the end of their session, she sent them on their way with a generous supply of free samples. The paying clients didn't get nearly as many goodies. In that instance we did not begrudge the "free lunch." As counter manager, I encouraged the absurd scene, and the instructrice and I felt as gratified as our wayward clients.

During one of the facial sessions, instructrice Linda informed me she got wind of my income. I don't know how she learned about it, and she wouldn't tell me. Linda could now add my "abundant" commissions to her long list of issues, topped by her back problems. She felt she deserved a higher income than mine – after all she had to lug from her car all the facial set-up equipment, including a heavy folding chair and screen, testers and Clarins products, as well as product stands. "Oh, my aching back!" (It's a given she could have asked for help).

While discussing my income and her hardships, I rested my hand on the counter. Linda actually pinched it! I yelled at her, and she said it was an accident. Right!

Linda was born in the United States but desperately wanted to be French, so she told everyone that she was. Did she think because she spent a week in Paris and wore Eiffel Tower earrings, she was entitled to French citizenship? Now and then she sprinkled mispronounced French words in her conversation with clients.

Linda's love for her Yorkie dog, Stella, bordered on idolatry. As soon as the clients sat in the reclining chair, she whipped out her scrapbook of Stella. The captive audience was then regaled with the Stella dog show, featuring tales of her adorable antics, her favorite foods, and yes, her amazing sense of humor. Linda's answering machine featured her voice punctuated with Stella's barks. I was disappointed that the dog didn't bark in French malapropisms like her "mom." Poor Stella – linguistically impaired!

In spite of small spats, Linda and I appreciated our individual personas. We worked well together, resulting in successful facial events, and were actually quite fond of each other.

EVENTFUL

My husband, Bernie, occasionally showed up at Bloomies to harass me. He mercilessly teased my associates, who loved it and gave it back to him in spades.

One day, while looking at the color display case, he pointed at the eye makeup, and said, "What's this?" Since he often watched me apply eye shadow in my bathroom mirror, I questioned his question. I asked Bernie if he wanted to make a purchase, but then my attention was drawn to one of my regular customers. At the completion of her purchase, I was ready to introduce her to Bernie.

I was aghast! When I finally turned my attention back to Bernie, both his eye contour areas were covered with cornflower blue eye shadow. The scene caused a riot of laughter among the associates. Ms. Wilcox the store manager, was close by, and her curiosity propelled her to the Clarins counter. I introduced her to my husband – what else could I do?

"I love that color on you," she told Bernie.

"Do you think this orange lipstick would go with it?" Bernie asked.

"I don't think it's bright enough – you need more color."

The crowd of Bernie fans among my co-workers joined in, and everyone had fun at the party. I advised Bernie that his antics meant he could look forward to having his despised broccoli for dinner that night.

The following week, Bernie appeared again.

A pretty young woman asked me for makeup

advice for her upcoming wedding "Why don't you have a seat and we can experiment with colors to go with your wedding dress, as well as colors for your honeymoon wardrobe." She was all for it.

Oh, oh, here comes trouble. As I reached for cotton squares, I saw Bernie walking towards me with a vigorous stride. I introduced him to the young lady and mentioned her impending marriage.

(What was I thinking?)

"What do you want to do that for?" Bernie said

"Why?" answered the unsuspecting customer.

"Have you any idea how miserable you're going to be? You're giving up your freedom and exchanging it for a hangover that never goes away."

"Bernie, please stop that," I ordered him

"Well, if married life is so awful, why are you still married?" the customer asked.

"It's cheaper to keep her," answered Bernie.

I retorted: "She's getting married, with or without your blessings. Don't you have somewhere to go?"

He addressed the future bride. "Do you know why husbands die before their wives?"

"No."

"Because they want to."

Bernie quickly changed his tune to one of sincerity. "Actually marriage is wonderful, he said. "Get married-why should you have it so good?" And with that, Bernie left.

The customer and I both laughed as I assured her that we are happily married to each other.

"Wale" of a Guy

Before leaving for work, I checked my schedule. *Oh good – Robert will be in today.*

At Bloomingdale's, we had our own celebrity – Robert Wale, makeup artist for Adrian Arpel. (Clarins shared the bay with Arpel). He was in his sixties but his vivacity and his playful and mischievous spirit belied his age. His face evidenced foundation, blush, eye shadow and mascara, and he had a full head of brown hair, peppered with gray. He proudly displayed a whale pin on his lapel and he looked altogether attractive. It was suicidal to address him as "Bob" if you wanted membership in his fan club. "My name is Robert," he would scornfully reply to the offender.

The women who occupied his chair looked up at him adoringly as he applied makeup. Each of his clients was treated to the same performance and makeup (one size fits all), and all ended up looking the same. He spewed out corny phrases, such as "There's hope with taupe" referred to old screen star magazines for makeup inspiration, and used gadgets, such as a miniature fan. The women were asked if they owned a mascara fan, and of course, none did.

"What! You don't own a mascara fan???"

Robert then dramatically whipped out his fan to dry their mascara. It took him about two hours to achieve the "look," and much of that time was not devoted to makeup application, but to his act which was a curtain raiser. The women loved the attention, the coddling, and sometimes, even the makeover.

Three days a month, Bob made his grand entrance, literally dancing in the aisles. The usual crowd of onlookers enjoyed the spectacle. The larger the crowd, the more outlandish his performance, as he basked in the attention. The customer on his vanity throne gloried as queen for a day. For the privilege, his "goddesses," as he referred to them spent big bucks.

One of his events was a classic. A woman arrived for the royal treatment. At the end of the two-hour session, Robert made his recommendation to help her make her product selection, and spend, spend, spend till the wallet cried.

"I'll have to think about it," she responded.

Robert was beside himself. He stopped breathing. In a fit of outrage, the killer whale grabbed a towel, plunged toward her and smeared his makeup masterpiece all over the woman's face, lipstick included.

The middle-aged matron looked ghastly and shrieked like a harpooned … well, whale. By far this was the best show in town!

Robert Wale was nearly fired for this stunt. That's showbiz, Kids.

Contests

Have you ever wondered about department store contests and if the outcome is always legitimate?

Well...I can only tell you about my experiences.

To entice shoppers, Clarins occasionally raffled off a basket of beauty aids, maybe worth over $200. Purchasers were eligible for the drawings; each received a numbered stub, which corresponded with their phone numbers left at the counter.

Time for the drawing. One at a time, my co-workers and I reached into the fish bowl full of stubs. Non-deserving (translation – poor spender). Next. Non-deserving, (she doesn't wear mascara). Next. Non-deserving, (she's *natural*.) Next. Non-deserving (she only buys hand cream).

Next. BINGO: The high roller won the prize.

Have fragrance customers wondered why the promised minitures in holiday gift sets have vanished? After all, these tiny sculptured fragrance bottles make ideal colectors' items. The miniatures and sets are safely stored in the stockroom. Did I say safely? Many fragrance emplyees collect the little gems and routinely lift them, somehow feeling a sense of entitlement—and the fragrance *manager* abetted the crime scenes. (Since I also collected miniatures, given the opportunity, I might have been tempted to follow suit.)

"What Happened?"

The month of February produced a major snowstorm that necessitated school closings and interruptions to business and life. The storm lasted several days, customers stayed away, and predictably, sales were low.

After the storm, the account executive arrived and scanned the sales report.

"What happened?" she asked incredulously. Apparently, even an act of G-d is no excuse for low sales. Whenever a Rouge Hag came in under quota, she was sure to have a stockpile of creative excuses at the ready. Here are some:

A customer took up all my time and spent nothing.

Lancôme was in "Gift."

My allergies acted up. (I have a lot of them).

Everyone was watching the ball game.

I was really sick (sick of work).

My front tooth fell out.

Does this remind you of grade school, as in the dog chewed up my homework?

CLARINS UNIFORMS

One of the Cosmetics Queens' favorite pastimes was to look in the mirrors, which were in abundance and strategically placed on counters. Was it our insecurity, a reflex response, or just plain vanity? I suspect, that for me, it was all three. This pastime might also include applying makeup and then reapplying it throughout the day. We bonded with the mirrors.

Periodically, we met for breakfast and some major gossiping. The muffins and coffee tasted so much better that way. On a particular morning, the gossip target was Annie. Her bay-mates referred to her as the refrigerator because she was short and walked with her hands glued to her side. She was the new kid on the block. How dare she try to make sales? Her co-workers saw to it that she spent her working hours mired in misery.

Annie wasn't on my mind that day; rather I was focused on the arrival of the long-promised new Clarins uniforms. After being subjected to a barrage of superlative descriptions, our high expectations landed with a thud. The uniforms turned out to be bright red polyester dresses with the ever-present French scarf. I don't know how bright red could be dowdy, but somehow Clarins had succeeded.

When I stood in front of the counter, I felt like a red tomato waiting for a bus. I tried to modify the look by keeping the dress unbuttoned - wearing it as a coat. I varied the look with T-shirts, sweaters, blouses, skirts and pants. It didn't fly with the vendor or staff. We were required to wear these fashion statements to all meetings and training school, while the trainers wore their stylish street clothes.

One day, I gave my Clarins uniform the day off. Wouldn't you know it, Mr. Horowitz, Sr., the U.S. president of the company, stopped by. Thankfully, recent sales were tops, which did not by any means get me off the hook. But it softened the blow for my noncompliance.

About a month after Mr. Horowitz's last visit, he appeared again, unannounced. He asked me if I would try to beat or at least match the sales volume of the nearby Prescriptives line. They did a high volume, and it didn't hurt them to be connected with Estee Lauder. The big attraction was their skin color matching technique and custom blended makeup.

The Prescriptives counter manager spoke with a lisp. Prescriptives is not an easy word to pronounce with a lisp. Try it.

Upon leaving the store, Mr. Horowitz said, "Marlit, would you please do me another favor and wear your uniform?" It was the second time he caught me. He was such a gentleman, and I truly felt ashamed.

INVENTORY

From a legal standpoint, inventory of store merchandise must be taken at least yearly. On-hand goods must be reconciled with those recorded in the system and inconsistencies corrected. An added perk: the entire store got a thorough cleaning and straightening.

Shortages discovered during the process of inventory were bad news. How did the shortages occur? It could be any number of reasons: pilferage by customers as well as employees, damages, errors in the system, sloppy record keeping, and employee indifference.

A form of pilferage: A friend of a sales associate makes a small purchase, while unpaid merchandise is also placed in the shopping bag.

Another form of pilferage: An associate spends an excessive amount of phone time at her counter conducting her part-time real estate business.

An over-the-top form of pilferage: A smartly dressed impeccably groomed, attractive forty-something female associate sells and steals shoes at Bloomingdale's. The aloof and hostile, shoe sales co-worker treated associates who purchased shoes from her with indifference. Periodically, at quitting time, she walked out of the door wearing new shoes from her department. They were not paid for. Eventually, she lost the game she played and was caught in the act. Two security officers escorted the handcuffed creature out the store, as the other sales associates gleefully watched.

****

Bloomingdale's was zealous about security. During training sessions, the newly hired were introduced to security officer Pat, who looked and was tough. Her intimidating stance was enough to scare anyone, but I saw a person that was direct and fair. She stood in front of the room and told us that she's the person to avoid. "I *love* to catch you doing something dishonest, and catch you I will. I'm everywhere."

Cameras were strategically placed in the cosmetics stockroom. A cosmetics associate was caught on camera leaving the stock room and store with a small piece of ribbon. Pat stopped her as she left the store. The employee explained that she wanted to use the ribbon to wrap a personal gift. The small piece of ribbon was worth pennies – if that much. But, Bloomies wanted to set an example and the hapless lady was fired. The following morning, at the cosmetics department meeting, Pat recounted the ribbon affair. It was her time to shine, and she milked it.

Tampering with the time clock was another form of pilferage. For example, someone would take a two-hour-plus lunch and only record one hour on the time clock, as a co-worker clocked the associate back in.

Upon leaving the store, you endured spot inspections. We were asked to open our purses as the staffer on duty peeked inside. At that time, they were not permitted to put their hands in the purses. It was not a thorough or efficient operation. Cosmetics testers, as well as live merchandise, were regularly hidden underneath purse paraphernalia, and the stolen items went undetected.

****

Eventually, the day of reckoning – inventory day – would come.

The store was open for business till 5-p.m., at which time inventory began. All employees were treated to a generous hot meal, served in shifts from 3 – 5 p.m. During inventory, snacks (chips, candy, drinks, cookies) were passed out.

At one time, the counting was done manually, in pairs. One person counted while the partner recorded the figures on paper. That method changed to using handheld devices to scan bar codes on merchandise.

Though most co-workers bitched about inventory, I saw it as a welcome break from the pressure of selling. The day after inventory was spent placing merchandise back in order. I overheard that some employees were fired or moved to other departments because of poor inventory performance.

THE NORDSTROM INVASION

The pending opening of a Nordstrom store in White Plains, New York, posed a threat for Bloomies. … real or imagined.

Bloomies pulled out all the stops to prepare for the invader. A professional training service was hired, and for two days, training classes were held at a nearby hotel. Former Nordstrom employees (spies) were invited to the sessions. The drill sergeants meant to whip us into shape and used films, props, music, tedious talks, and cheerleader tactics. We even did role playing and sing-a-longs.

The trainer asked for role-playing volunteers, so I lowered my eyes, foolishly hoping to become invisible. The ploy didn't work for me in grade school and it didn't work for me here. My bright striped blouse didn't help. I should have forgotten to wear my nametag.

"Marlit, come on up, honey," the trainer said.

I was assigned the role of the difficult customer and the other role - player was the salesperson.

Me: I have to return this.

She: Oh, I'm sorry, is there a problem?

Me: Yes, I'm unhappy with the cream I bought from you. It didn't do anything.

She: Well, what did you want it to do?

Me: Not only didn't your firming cream not firm, but it did nothing for my lines.

She: This isn't plastic surgery you know.

Me: How dare you – are you implying that I need

plastic..........

Trainer: All right, all right – thank you ladies – you may sit down.

At the conclusion of the session, we were required to complete written examinations. We were never informed about the test results.

Thoroughly trained, but none the wiser, we returned to Bloomingdale's where we were greeted with a 50" x 60" sign on the employees entrance wall.

YES, I CAN.

It is said competition is good for business. In my opinion the hotel training sessions were time wasters for the associates, and money wasters for Bloomingdale's. Once the Nordstrom store opening excitement blew over, Bloomingdale's store traffic was quite healthy, as was also the case for my own counter business.

But I did enjoy browsing in Nordstrom's during my lunch hour.

A FOND FAREWELL

I felt pressure (mostly self-inflicted) to improve my sales performance, so I decided to get out of cosmetics and perhaps switch to fashion. Or maybe I'd get out of retail altogether. I felt that I needed to reach the high performance bar I continually raised for myself, and to do otherwise would let Bloomies, Clarins and myself down.

I did not have to anguish long over this dilemma. The decision was made for me when my husband and I opted to move to Cleveland, Ohio. After six glorious (and occasionally maddening) years at Bloomingdale's I gave my two weeks notice. I would sure miss the place.

COMMUNIQUE

Marlit Polsky, Counter Manager at Bloomingdale's, White Plains, New York was given that store's award for outstanding salesmanship and service. Not only did she bring CLARINS business up +49% for the year, but she also had the highest percent increase of all the store's employees!

I had received many awards and accolades during my half-dozen years at Bloomies. Flowers and candy delivered to my counter to show recognition and appreciation for high sales and successful facial events, as well as numerous acknowledgements. My most outstanding award was for the 49% increase in Clarins business over a six-month period. It was the highest sales increase during that period in the entire store, and I was awarded $100, gifts, trinkets, dinner for two at their wonderful restaurant, as well as a celebrity parking space. In addition, an award breakfast in my honor was held in the restaurant before it opened for customer business.

With my resignation, I found myself in the party spotlight again. My co-workers planned a surprise for me. But thanks to one of my friends in the department, the surprise was never really a surprise. "Big mouth" revealed the date and time so that I would know to dress up for the big day. No Rouge Hag wants to be caught underdressed! My friend's intentions were honorable.

So, dress up I did. I also brought along a stack of 8" x 10" black-and-white glossies of myself, leftovers from my voice-over acting days.

Upon hearing of my resignation, Arlene, the Arden counter manager who had given me lots of grief in the past, suddenly became my best friend. Now she rejoiced when I had a big sale, shared her snacks, bared her personal secrets, and was downright euphoric at my impending departure.

The party took place in the cosmetics department manager's office during work hours, and I was summoned on a pretext. I might not have looked surprised as I entered, but I'm certain that I looked genuinely happy and excited. To assure counter coverage, my co-workers arrived in segments.

A co-worker's husband supplied scrumptious food from his Italian restaurant. David, who worked in fragrances, baked a marvelous strawberry cake with my name on top. The department gifted me with a beautiful

Marlit (third from left) receiving Bloomingdale's Award for Outstanding Service.

61

pin and earring set. The jewelry was accompanied with a greeting card signed by my co-workers, who roasted me.

I was truly flattered and grateful. My heart was full.

But now it was my turn. I distributed my pictures to the group as they stood in line for autographs.

"Leave it to Marlit to pull a stunt like this," my co-workers laughed. After all, what's more presumptuous and obnoxious than to give presents of a picture of oneself?

MARLIT POLSKY

PART 2

DILLARD'S

DILLARD'S

Cleveland is not New York. Dillard's is not Bloomingdale's.

I planned to stay in the workforce, but again, I wanted a position that was socially oriented.

Dillard's held the counter manager position for me for two months. Clarins management asked me to stay on board because of Eric's directive.
The Dillard's job interview was brief: "We are very happy to have you."

What struck me about my new workplace was the lack of store traffic. I thought, *I will be bored into a coma.* Also, the customers were of a different breed. New York customers made a purchase without much soul searching. The Cleveland customers agonized about a purchase.

Dillard's department store was situated in Beachwood Place shopping mall. Shopping malls are an American institution, as much about restaurants, food courts, and entertainment events, as they are about shopping. And then there are the mall walkers, who arrive in large numbers for their exercise fix. It was going to be a whole new world for this Cosmetics Queen.

THE DILLARD'S WAY

The Dillard's pay system had a built-in failure component. Often, unrealistic sales per hour (SPH) amounts had to be met or a 10% pay cut resulted. If the SPH was met, the employees kept their hourly wage. If the SPH was exceeded, a 10% raise was given. A soft economy, merchandise shortage, adverse weather, or too many salespeople in a given area were not accepted as excuses for low sales.

The yearly or six-month review was summed up in one word – numbers. In my department, nothing was mentioned about customer service, product knowledge, sales competence or grooming. We manned the counters, did stock work, worked the telephones and performed all the tasks necessary to maintain the work area. It's a given that we make sales. The associates vigorously complained about the pay cuts, which resulted in substantial turnovers.

Some employees bucked the system. When reviews loomed and pay cuts were threatened, they rang up sales for each other, expecting the favor to be returned. Some asked friends or relatives to make huge purchases from other areas and bring the merchandise to them to ring up. After the review, the items were returned.

In addition to pay cuts, other store maneuvers decreased the paycheck. Seasonal products, like sun lotions, self-tanners, and body products, were positioned in strategic areas in the store, such as the bathing suit and lingerie department. It's a smart and expedient move to increase department store sales. Those who worked for the mega cosmetics lines weren't seriously affected.

I was irritated when Sandy from the swimwear department repeatedly helped herself to Clarins sun products at my counter, some of which were in short supply. Sandy and other non-Clarins salespeople who still rang Clarins sales, found the increase in their paychecks. This practice lasted through the summer. Clarins sun and body products did a brisk seasonal business, but those of us at the Clarins counter didn't fully benefit.

There were other strategies employees used to pad their sales. Some didn't hesitate to ring sales from nearby counters if the legitimate associate was in the process of ringing another sale. Accusations and denials flew from all directions.

But a worse scenario of a different nature occurred when security persons accompanied dismissed (fired) employees to the manager's office to be informed that they were no longer needed. They gathered their personal belongings and then were exposed to the humiliation of being seen by co-workers as security escorted them out the door.

It wasn't all survival of the fittest. Co-workers often performed thoughtful deeds for each other. Observing from afar a co-worker doing a makeover, we casually walked over and complimented the associate on her artistic color application skills. Then we turned our attention to the customer in the chair and gushed about her radiant and wonderful new look. So, we lied a little. What's a little white lie if it helps a friend make a sale?

But it's also easy to lose a sale. While stocking sun products, a young lady stopped by and asked for a bright lipstick to go with her Florida tan. She had just graduated from high school and was planning a Florida vacation. "You should consider an S.P.F of at least 15," I said. "You have beautiful but delicate skin and you need good protection from the Florida sun." Clarins sun products with an S.P.F. of at least 15 or 20 have a built-in tanning accelerator, and you'd get a more intense tan than if you used nothing."

"You sound just like my mother."

Oh, oh, I just lost a sale. "Would you like to look at a lipstick? We can come back to the sun lotion."

"No, that's okay." She left.

The Counter Princess

My first day at Dillard's was full of surprises, one being the Clarins associate, I had to supervise.

What a pretty girl – that was my first impression of Jennifer. Her claim to fame, was keeping company with the Clarins Midwest sales manager's son. She felt that the "dating game" conferred special privileges. Her perception was correct. The staff and many co-workers treated her like a princess, especially the Dillard's store manager. Although I was counter manager, he only acknowledged Jennifer, the part-timer, with "Good Mornings" and business situations, while he ignored me. I felt slighted and insulted.

After a month settling in at Dillard's, it was time to deal with Jennifer. I did not buy into the noblesse oblige granted her because of her significant other. Her mode of operation was to do as little work as she could get away with. She had phenomenal phone stamina and I asked her to keep her personal calls to a reasonable number. I also made it clear to her that she was expected to do her share of stock work, cleaning, and other chores that kept the counter working profitably and efficiently.

She was angry and caught off balance and fought back with senseless ranting.

"I had no problem until you came here!"

"You're not going to boss me around just because you're counter manager!"

"Everyone here likes me!"

"I know the Clarins line better than you do!"

She finished her outburst, and then stopped talking to me for a week. That was a good week.

Shortly after our head-on collision, Jennifer began to comply with my requests and carried out her responsibilities competently and cheerfully. Perhaps she realized that while she may be a princess, I was still the counter queen. In due time, we learned to co-exist and to respect and have affection for each other.

Eventually, the store manager announced his forthcoming departure due to ill health. He shook hands to bid farewell to some of the employees, including me. He ignored Jennifer. I suspected that he felt relieved to finally be authentic.

When Jennifer resigned for a position in the financial field, we ended our cosmetics alliance on a high note with many hugs. I'll admit, I missed her presence at the counter.

Her boyfriend eventually became her husband and also store manager at an out-of town Dillard's. At last count, they had two children.

I suppose that's a real fairy tale.

Storewide

Dillard's regularly conducted a storewide meeting before business hours. The employees were notified that attendance was "mandatory." The staff *loved* to use that word. High-sugar doughnuts, juice, and coffee were served. Many employees staggered in without having had breakfast, so they didn't care *what* they ate.

Much business was crammed in at the hourly morning meetings.

Monthly and yearly sales figures were compared to those of the previous year. Top employee performers were recognized. Complimentary letters from customers were read, and prizes awarded to those mentioned in these letters.

1.   Promotions for mangers or employees were announced.

2.   Sometimes the department managers modeled new clothes or displayed new items.

3.   The yearly "Pacesetters" were introduced. Pacesetters had the highest sales, and were rewarded with a dinner party and special nametags.

4.   Department mangers performed skits during the holidays. A Santa was always present at Christmas time.

5.   Numbered tickets were distributed upon arrival at the meetings. The randomly drawn winning numbers received Dillard's gift certificates, store merchandise, or a lottery ticket.

6.   Most employees participated enthusiastically in the dog and pony show. Most also needed their jobs.

(Mis) MANAGEMENT

According to most Dillard's employees, executive or managerial job applicants had to be endowed with specific attributes: rudeness, poor temper, no sense of humor, and just flat-out nastiness. I found that employees' comfort level is predicated, in part, on the smarts and good (or not so good) will of store and department managers.

"Have you heard the buzz?, Hannah is out."

Hannah was the manager of our flagship store. In a letter posted near the time clock, she explained, "For personal reasons, I am leaving the store to become store manager of another store."

The employees concluded it must be a less prestigious and smaller Dillard's.

Hannah was small in physical stature but huge with emotional baggage. It was common knowledge that this "walking neurosis" screamed at her department managers at the daily inspirational morning meetings. Her signature was a perpetual frown, as she turned her head the other way when an associate passed her.

Inventory and Hannah were not compatible. She ordered bathroom doors locked, forcing employees to ask for permission to use the facilities. Talking or whispering was not only frowned on, but incited her to scream.

One late inventory night, while on the prowl, Hannah screamed and yelped at a young man who was resting and ordered him to go back to work. He replied, "You are not my mother and I don't like you to scream at me."

"I am not your mother but your boss," Hannah retorted. "You're fired."

She liked the Clarins treatments and frequently came behind the counter to help herself to a generous amount of samples, even though she knew we were only given a small monthly supply.

In my book, there are high expectations of a flagship store manager's behavior, and Hannah's pursuit of self-gratification was a disappointment.

She did have a kind streak that surfaced periodically. For example, when some merchandise fell to the floor and she noticed a senior associate attempting to pick it up, Hannah stopped her and sent a young fluff chick to do the job. She also had a sympathetic heart for the new kid on the block. Many of the existing sales personnel did not welcome new employees with open arms. Under Hannah's watch, new arrivals were to be treated kindly, given adequate help, and made to feel welcome. She threatened that failure to comply with her decree was grounds for termination. This rule was not really enforced. I never knew of a case where termination resulted.

I asked for Hannah's permission to attend my niece's New York wedding.

"You know that in November and December, you cannot take vacation days because of holiday traffic," she said. "I'm sorry, but I can't allow this."

I thanked her for her time, went on the trip, and nothing was ever mentioned about the incident.

★★★★

Two days after Hannah's departure from the flagship store, George, the new store manager, arrived on the scene. He was young, in his forties, cute looking, with an open, cheerful personality. He shook hands as he introduced himself to all the employees and engaged them in friendly conversation. A co-worker said to me, "This guy is like a glass of ice water on a hot day."

I agreed that George was a welcome change, after dour and frowning Hannah. However, the Cosmetics Queens were not pushovers, so we postponed our evaluation pending further evidence.

Alas, many employees were fired soon after George's arrival, so we tagged him "the Sweeper," here to clean house. Personally, I appreciated his take-charge approach. I thought that a house cleaning was overdue, and if the store were run more efficiently, better sales would result, thereby benefiting the employees.

A thorough cleansing was also in order for our security crew. Security in our store was a joke. During the years I worked at Dillard's, an astonishing number of incidents occurred. A fire was started in the lingerie department while the perpetrators walked out of the store with armloads of leather jackets. Where were the guards? A reasonable question. Luckily, an alert associate called the fire department, and the damage was limited.

Most mall stores closed on Saturday at 7:30 p.m. Dillard's stayed open until 9. One associate dubbed us Gangland, U.S.A. On one such Saturday night, a huge amount of Gucci watches were lifted. Again, where was security? Pilferage is routine in the retail business, but a lot of the theft that took place at Dillard's could have been avoided. The security guards were more interested in flirting with the pretty young girls than chasing crooks. Many security personnel were eventually swept out of their jobs.

At Dillard's, cameras were strategically placed throughout the store. Whether or not a theft was observed and recorded on camera, often just the mention of our electronic partners scared the crooks into confessions.

After George sought to make an impact on security, he turned his attention to another terrible blight at Dillard's: sitting. Sitting down while working was not permitted. The absence of a break, other than dinner or lunch, often left the associates in a state of fatigue, and their legs felt like phantom appendages. The urge to sit, if only for a few minutes, was often irresistible. Helene had that urge when she sat on a chair in *front* of her counter. These chairs were placed for the customers' convenience. Two days into his new position, George appeared and asked Helene what she was doing. Wide-eyed Helene's limp excuse was, "I had an accident and fell into the chair."

His reply: "If you were on the floor, I'd believe you.

George caught two housewares department employees sitting down ten minutes before closing time when no customers were around. One of the employees told me that he screamed at them, as his face became beet red.

George was of help to me concerning a situation at Clinique, my next-door neighbor. Clinique had often been a splinter under my nail, even back at Bloomingdale's.

To promote their fragrance "Happy," the song, "Get Happy" was played repeatedly at high volume. The constancy and loudness of the noise pollution unraveled me. Even after I left the store, the tune still played in my head. Because of the proximity, it was a supreme nuisance when I tried to converse with customers. The medical establishment has proven that noise is a threat to good health and emotional well-being. I tried to reason with Ali, the Clinique counter manager.

"Ali, please do me a favor and turn down the volume of the Get Happy song, or at least periodically shut if off. The loudness makes it difficult to work with my customers," I said in the friendliest manner I could.

"Sorry," Ali replied. "My boss wants it on a high volume. Why don't you take your customers to the far end of your counter? I'm not going to discuss this any further with you."

Finally, I could no longer tolerate the audio harassment and marched myself into George's office. I pleaded my cause and told him I could not work at my counter under the present condition. He promised me that he would take care of it – and he did. I spotted him that same day talking to the Clinique manager. The audio player was moved to the far side, away from the Clarins counter, and the volume was considerably lowered. I was always able to solve petty problems with associates, but this time I felt backed into a corner.

My feelings toward Clinique were not only those of vexation. I have several fond memories of my Clinique bay mates. I couldn't hold a grudge against them because business was great at their counter. Also, the account executive told me how grateful she was when I helped Clinique at a time they were shorthanded during a promotion. She handed me a bag filled with Clinique products.

After George had been with my store for about two years, he was assigned to another store for a manager position. In spite of his sporadic mean streak, I was sorry to see him go. He treated me with respect and sometimes even overlooked my waywardness. When applicable, he went out of his way to inform employees that he appreciated their efforts.

****

If I were at a watch tower detached from Dillard's, I'd enjoy the outstanding theatre that was Chrissie. We were warned about Chrissie, our new cosmetics manager. She had a reputation for bizarre behavior from her previous position at another Dillard's store.

She visited each cosmetics counter upon her arrival. There was not getting to know you chitchat. Her greeting to me was, "I will be checking your sales numbers every day." She delivered on that promise.

Her good looks and get-ups were showstoppers. She had a beautiful face, extraordinary blue eyes, and a petite yet curvy figure. Her blond, highlighted hair extensions cascaded down her back to her waist and were adorned with decorative hairpieces. She always sported a tan with the help of tanning booths and tanning products. Chrissie was never seen without boots, whether in a skirt or trousers, winter or summer (even under her wedding gown). Beads and sequins were prominent on her outfits. She wore shoulder-length earrings, faux furs around the neck, and an abundance of jewels.

I eagerly anticipated her look of the day. Her dress mode was original and great fun, however inappropriate. It belonged in a juke joint, nightclub, or at a party, especially since the other employees were required to observe a dress code.

At morning "pep rallies," led by Chrissie, we were subjected to insults and sarcasm. The entire cosmetics group was privy to our personal daily sales figures with special emphasis on low sales. Our attire and makeup were criticized and ridiculed. When she singled me out, I answered her back in kind.

"Marlit, when are you going to change your lipstick color?"

"When my lips start complaining."

"New shoes, Marlit?"

"The store was out of yellow boots," I answered.

One day in passing, she said to me, "you stink," because my sales had gone south. Another time, she commented about my low sales for that day. I mumbled a lame excuse and she answered, "Get me a puke bucket."

Chrissie presided over professionally run cosmetics business meetings. Momentarily, I was inspired and full of respect for her, but soon my feelings evaporated as she conducted business as usual on the cosmetics floor.

For one weekend, the store had a special shoppers event and formal dress was the expected attire. She encouraged the ladies to borrow long formal eveningwear from the Dillard's dress department. We were also encouraged to borrow boa feathers, formal jewelry, and shoes.

"Won't we get into trouble?" The ladies asked.

The party animal answered, "Just help yourselves – take anything you want."

We had a screaming good time, and as a group, we looked pretty darned good. I wondered how she pulled it off, after the worn outfits (complete with sweat stains, food stains, tears) were returned to the proper departments.

Chrissie did have a caring and soft side. She saw

to it, when possible, we were not subjected to pay cuts. This gesture endeared her to us.

Chrissie was daring and non-conformist. She added vibrancy and sparkle to the department. For a while she got away with her antics because department sales were high. I had a secret admiration for her irreverence. Ultimately, she left the store for another job. This light had dimmed for me. Indeed, the light had dimmed in the cosmetics department.

****

We had complained about George the "Sweeper." After he was gone, we wished he were back.

Elliot, the new store manager, seemed harmless at first. If his reputation hadn't preceded him, we would have thought him to be a pushover.

We didn't have to wait long for the substance of the man to emerge. He only acknowledged our existence by barking at us. Otherwise, no "Good morning," or "How are you?" or even "Drop dead."

He suffered from SMS – short man's syndrome. The employees assigned him names: Caesar, Little Man, Daddy, and also some unmentionables.

He was a rather nice looking man, probably in his late forties, fair complected, medium blond hair, and sporting a mustache. One morning he made his store entrance exhibiting orange hair, although he quickly changed it back to its original color.

Few fathers would yell at their children the way Daddy yelled at the sales associates. In addition to screaming, he banged his fists. One unfortunate associate, who for some reason fueled his rage, endured a chair being thrown against his office wall. Two cosmetics sales associates were fired on the spot when he saw them in the shoe department on company time.

One early morning, from my bedroom window, I saw the trees doing their wind dance. The sky was dark and moody. *I must go to work. I must get out of bed.* I had forebodings that were soon to be realized. I ran to the employee entrance door to avoid being late. Although I heard no sounds, I was acutely aware of being followed. I reached the door, turned around, and there was Daddy. I was already breathless from running, but at the sight of him, I hyperventilated.

"You're not allowed to park where you did. Go move your car."

"I have a pass that allows me to park in this section," I explained. "It's in the personnel office."

"I'll check it out," he said.

Elliot stopped at my counter later that day.

"I didn't know you have a pass. Don't forget the pass has to be renewed every six months." I thanked him. I took Elliot's remarks for the closest I could get to an apology.

At Christmas time, wearing a Santa hat and a huge smile, Elliot visited the employees at their work stations and gave each a candy cane and a plastic lunch bag. He enjoyed this activity. For Thanksgiving, Dillard's treated the employees to a delicious hot turkey dinner with all the trimmings. With a chef hat and apron in place, Daddy served the food. He was full of good cheer. It was a pleasure to see him in this light.

Saturdays, he usually walked the floor at a frantic pace to check on the workers. He repeated these walks over and over again, like a man possessed. One day, he walked near my counter, with a paper bag from the mall food court. The irresistible smell of fries prompted me to ask him if I could have a bite. He made a primal sound.

Elliot ran a tight operation, and the store was doing well. It was hard to argue with success.

I once sat next to the display gal in the employee dining room. She had worked with Elliot for many years at the Beachwood store, as well as at another Dillard's store, and had only high praise for him. Another employee had a similar high opinion of him when she was a buyer at another store. These testimonials show the complexity of the man. One day as I passed Daddy in the hall, he cheerfully said hello to me *twice*. He also stopped frantically pacing the store and went out of his way to be cordial to employees.

What's going on? I wondered.

OFF THE CHARTS

Employees were encouraged to promote their skincare cosmetics lines over the PA, which could be heard throughout the store. The associates enjoyed listening to themselves on the loudspeaker, but most of the messages were about as exciting as a dial tone.

Earlier in my career I had plunked down one thousand greenbacks for voice-over lessons, and they would now be put to use. I delivered a series of messages that got the ear of the customers as well as the associates. I began each message with attention-getters, followed with hype for a particular product:

"Oh no - cellulite! Are you unaware of your cellulite? Others may not be."

"Do you stay awake because of cellulite? Get your cellulite fix at the Clarins counter and get some sleep tonight."

"Do you have cellulite? Well you're not special – 85% of women have it. No need to join a support group."

"Did you hear the one about the traveling salesman? The salesman stopped at a farmhouse – oh, never mind. Sometimes jokes are funny, but having cellulite is no joke."

These announcements were followed by invitations to the Clarins counter to help solve their problems.

And then I tried these:

"Have you spent quality time with your mirror lately?"

"Are looks everything? Of course not – they're the only thing."

"Attention ladies! Have you tried our famous neck cream? It's for everyone who has a neck. Have you tried our fabulous bust lotion? Don't get me started. Come see me at the Clarins counter."

"It's no sin to be ugly – just stay home. OR stop by to try the new Clarins color collection."

I felt uneasy as soon as I spewed out that final provocative message. But, something propelled me, and I charged ahead. I no sooner hung up the phone to the PA system, when Elliot called.

"I don't like that announcement" he grunted, "It's not funny and it's not professional – I don't want to hear this kind of thing again."

I had to agree – he had a point. But I was disturbed about Elliot's phone call. The truth is for those who can handle it.

Did Elliot want me to stop *all* announcements? He wasn't clear about it, and I wasn't about to confront him. I decided that my broadcasting career at Dillard's was over. My creativity was not appreciated.

Customers and associates badgered me to continue with the announcements. I wasn't required to do this, and after Elliot's put-down, I would have felt intimidated. Besides the fun was now taken out of it.

INVENTORY FROM HELL

Dillard's semi-annual inventory was a shameful, two-day occurrence, and the foreplay began many days before the event. For days, merchandise was sorted, labeled, cleaned and folded, and after inventory, it had to be put back in its proper place.

The morning shift began at 5:30 a.m. and ended at 3 p.m. The night shift was from 3,4, or 5 p.m., ending someday between 1-4 a.m. I chose my poison and selected the early bird special. The previous night's sleep was always sporadic and restless, if one could sleep at all. Upon arriving at 5:30 a.m., we were treated to high-sugar, high-fat doughnuts and a java jolt.

The inventory fashion show was a revelation. Some arrived in dress clothes enhanced with copious accessories. It was an opportunity to prove they had a wardrobe, since many departments mandated uniforms. Some arrived for the morning shift sans makeup. This was a departure from their usual overly made-up faces. One gal always wore a sports cap backwards. The farmer masquerading as a beauty consultant arrived in denim overalls, slippers, and pigtails.

One year, Dillard's had an all-night inventory, which resulted in several injuries and illnesses. Upon leaving the store at 6:30 a.m., an associate crashed her car into an employee's station wagon in the parking lot. It was apparent that this experiment was a colossal failure. It resulted in inaccurate counting, serious complaints and physical problems. The all-nighter was abandoned. The morning shift was also eliminated, leaving us all stuck with 3 p.m. to early morning.

Inventory injuries were commonplace – tripping, falling, bumping, bruising, headaches and sprains. One year, I became a casualty, when two days of scanning, followed by a day of using a pricing gun, resulted in a hand/arm injury.

At times, employees asked to leave before the evening's end. All were denied this request. Being tired was not an excuse. *Nothing* was accepted as an excuse to leave early.

During one inventory, all outside doors were locked. An employee called the fire department, (We were on familiar terms with them), and the fire marshal arrived shortly. He made it clear that Dillard's faced a serious violation for locking us in, and if they ever tried this stunt again, they would be slapped with an immense fine.

One year, the cosmetics department manager was getting married, but her boss informed her she had to delay her honeymoon because she had inventory duty. Only death is accepted as an excuse. She chose life and quit.

One time, a mistake on the printed schedule stated the shift ended at midnight. During inventory, the store manager asked those who were on this schedule to stay till 1 a.m., but three employees had made previous arrangements to be picked up at 12. In total twelve employees clocked out at midnight. When that dirty dozen returned to work, after inventory, they discovered that they were out of a job.

THE ODD COUPLE

Many employees tackled their job only for the paycheck, but sales associate Amy carried her disdain for work to an extraordinary degree. She easily put in a full day's work at the store doing nothing.

Amy was in her mid-thirties, cute, outgoing, clever, and fun. I believed these attributes had enabled her to outfox the manger for several years.

She *was* terrific with customers, telling each one that the item they were considering was her personal favorite. When she was "on," her sales were high.

Amy planned her workday around Daddy's schedule. Immediately after she arrived, she called the switchboard operator to check on the store manager's attendance. If he was present for the day, she arranged her social activities on the phone. This killed two birds – she looked busy and professional and got her social calendar in order. Daddy's days off were cause for celebration, and Amy spent little time at the counter.

Waiting for merchandise to go on sale, she hid the items in drawers behind the counter – sometimes for weeks.

She enjoyed taking a bath in self-tanning lotion. On her days off, she attended cosmetics meetings dressed in short shorts and a halter. I suspected that the fashionista came to the meetings to show off her streaked tan, rather than to become informed. Plus, she was paid for the time.

Amy and I shared a ride to one of the Clarins schools. She was the driver and negotiated the steering wheel with her knee, racing all the time. We were still late and missed a portion of the meeting.

As expected, Elliot tortured her. He screamed at her in his office and even in the mall when he suspected her to be slacking while on the clock. Amy was convinced Daddy had a hidden camera in his office beamed directly at her. Why else would he always show up where she was?

I teased her that Elliot had the hots for her. My bay mates and I referred to them as "the love birds."

We wondered how she managed to be chronically absent from work and get away with it. Finally, the mystery was solved. After each absence, she presented her doctor's note to personnel. Dillard's required a doctor's note to validate illness and absences. Wasn't her doctor tired of supplying her with what seemed like an endless stream of excuse letters? There was a reason why he wasn't tired—he was deceased! Amy's friend had her late physician father's signature stamp along with a supply of letterheads.

Amy made frequent trips to Elliot's office to explain away her antics and face the inevitable reprimands. The associates felt he was itching to find concrete evidence to legally justify her termination. This missing piece to the Amy puzzle had eluded him.

"What will I do if he calls me into his office again? I can't take it anymore," Amy asked her co-workers. One of them suggested she should imagine that Elliot was naked and then report back to us what she saw. I told Amy, "You know he has a thing for you. He'll never fire you! He's having too much fun."

My intuition was wrong! After much blood hounding, Elliot finally nailed Amy. She was escorted out the front door by security. The associates were not privy to information as to why she was let go.

Amy's departure saddened the cosmetics associates. She may not have been a model employee, but her shenanigans provided us with many laughs. I enjoyed her wild capers and would miss her scheduled "emergencies."

Good-Bye Elliot

The pieces to the puzzle concerning Elliot's new positive attitude, began to fit. An employee sent a letter to Elliot's boss, which stated that an employee class action suit, as well as media notification, concerning Elliot's abuse of employees was forthcoming. Elliot was given two weeks to stop the harassment, threats and the outrageous behavior directed at employees.

Ultimately, Elliot left to become store manager of Dillard's in Chandler, Arizona, and I learned that he's very happy.

Maybe the desert heat cooled him off.

TAPESTRY OF CO-WORKERS

Like Bloomies, Dillard's was home to a colorful array of characters.

There were the spritzers – associates who would hand perfume-drenched cards to customers to try and sell a fragrance. Some over zealous spritzers converged on customers and directly sprayed them. Those pushy souls asked for trouble, and trouble they got – bringing down the wrath of unhappy shoppers. Some customers went as far as to threaten lawsuits, and some even made good on their threats. Many people are allergic to fragrances, but truthfully, many didn't want to be approached with a sales pitch in any form.

A fragrance spritzer once regaled me with her favorite customer malapropisms, like the one who wanted Anais-Anais and asked for "anus-anus." Or the Chanel seeker who pronounced it "channel". Or the unfortunate soul who called Organza fragrance "orgasm."

Spritzers are a unique community in that they make up their own rules. They did not ring up sales for themselves, but many handed business to their favorite salespersons, rather than dividing sales equally among the gals. Major conniving was required in order to become the pet of a spritzer. It fostered tensions for the losers in this game. Management seemed to be indifferent and focused on the bottom line – sales.

Let me stress that I have met many fine and noble spritzers whom I would be proud to call my friend—especially those who donated "miniatures" (tiny fragrance bottles) for my personal collection.

Spritzers loved to parade their potions near

cosmetics counters. Many lines sold their own fragrances and resented the competition. One of the spritzers stalked the Clarins counter, doing her fragrance shtick, gradually becoming bolder. My co-worker and my reproving looks didn't faze her. The middle aged, overly made-up spritzer wore tight-fitting, low-cut clothes to flaunt her ample bosom (or its synthetic equivalent). She wildly waved perfume soaked cards in customers' faces.

One day, she shamelessly addressed my customer, handing her a fragrance card while she was checking out Clarins testers. I was in the process of finishing a sale. After the customer concluded her business with me, I confronted the spritzer.

"From where did you get your nerve? Did you go to a special school?"

"You don't tell me what to do! I can do whatever I want."

"That's right," I said. "You can do whatever you want. Just don't do it near my counter."

She never did again.

Sex Sells

Kelly flew into Dillard's and landed at the Clarins counter.

I became privy to my new bay mate's soap opera life within three seconds of meeting her. Kelly, in her forties had a gorgeous face, a voluptuous body, and flaming long red hair, and she flaunted it all. Who can blame her? She resembled Ann Margaret.

During Christmas time, Kelly showed me a 5" x 9" picture of herself sitting on Santa's lap. In addition to parading the picture at the cosmetics counters, she also shoved it in the customers' faces.

One day, she stopped two handsome men. I wondered – now what is she up to? I didn't have to wait long to find out. She asked if either had a wife or girlfriend, as she tossed her hair in their faces. She then suggested they buy the Clarins bust gel to keep women's breasts firm. "Think about it – wouldn't you enjoy helping the ladies apply the gel?" The men looked at her sideways, thanked her, and walked away.

"Do you sing to your husband?" she asked me one day. "I always sing to my boyfriend."

"I sing in the shower, but not to my husband," I replied.

"Take him in the shower with you."

"Come on, let's sing," Kelly persisted. "Do you know Unchained Melody?"

"Sure I do."

We began to sing: "Oh, my love, my darling. I hunger for your touch" . . . She then spoiled the sweet moment: "Do you notice how the men stare at me?"

"Of course I do," I admitted.

Kelly was self-absorbed. A conversation was only relevant if it focused on her.

"Don't you think that hairstyle would look good on me?"

"That color is perfect for me."

"I can carry off clinging clothes."

If she keeps this up, I will throw up on her head, I thought.

At a special evening selling event, we were asked to dress up. Kelly made her entrance in a black, off-the-shoulder fur-trimmed dress. In addition, she draped a feather boa over her shoulder, which she waved at the male customers. The boa was shedding black feathers all over the place. She often complained that this line of work didn't hold enough excitement for her. I didn't know how much longer she could last with Clarins. I didn't know how much longer I could last with *her*.

The Drunken Diva

When Lydia clocked in, she lost no time beginning her ritual. She worked her way from one cosmetics counter to another to give herself a complete makeover, which took her anywhere from forty-five minutes to one hour. She had a heavy hand with colors. Her blond bangs stood at attention, and the punk hairdo made for an incongruous appearance. Lydia, in her thirties was attractive and didn't need these extremes.

Lydia was on close terms with the bottle and often came to work inebriated. At times, she was so off- balance, that she couldn't work the cash register. She explained it away, blaming it on medication for her back problem. One day, a true meltdown occurred when she tipsied into the stock room and fell while climbing a ladder. The ambulance arrived, and with much fanfare, she was carted away on a gurney. The accident necessitated a three-week absence.

Paula, the cosmetics manager at the time, was aware of Lydia's on-going problem and asked me to report to her when Lydia was high or drunk. I'm not an informer and never blew the whistle on her. Looking back, maybe I should have ratted on her – it might have spared her grief.

When Lydia returned to work she was placed in Siberia – the lingerie department – which we all tried to avoid because it was flat-out messy.

It was hard to dismiss Lydia's friendliness, vulnerability, and charisma. She was blissfully unaware of her conduct, which added to her charm.

She flirted with anything that resembled a man. She entertained us with wild tales of her mall lunch break conquests.

Dillard's was in the midst of its remodeling project, and the store teemed with construction workers. Some women fall in love with men in uniforms – apparently, hard hats did it for Lydia. Her makeup became more theatrical and stories of her new paramours became more outlandish.

The story has a fairy tale ending. A construction worker fell for the drama that was Lydia, and within a few months, they were married.

She's No. 1

Without a doubt, Liz reigned supreme in the fragrance department. Was it her magnetic personality, her energy, or the demands she placed on herself? Liz always had been No.1 in sales in the fragrance, as well as the cosmetics department.

She beguiled the customers and went out of her way for them. At holiday time, especially Christmas, the customers were seen carting away fragrance-filled shopping bags one on each hand. The store executives were thrilled with Liz's performance and allowed her great leeway to handle transactions.

Periodically, Middle Eastern heads of state visited the world renowned Cleveland Clinic for medical diagnoses and procedures. They often visited the store with their entourage. The women, accompanied by their chaperones, headed for the fragrance department. The visitors spent mega bucks, and Liz, who had spent time and effort to seduce them, handled almost all purchases.

This profound success incited hostility and envy among the associates who worked with Liz; even those who didn't work with her grew irritated. Many disagreements and some downright fights occurred. Some, who couldn't handle the competition, asked to be transferred. The resident fragrance neurotic completely lost it one day after a blow-up about whose customers "belong" to whom. She quit on the spot.

But Liz just kept on selling. Eventually Liz's reign was toppled at the fragrance department. She was moved to designer dress wear, where she remained wildly successful.

My 'Gift Box'

"Hi, I'm Margo. I'll be working with you at the Clarins counter. Ahchoo! Ahchoo!"

"Do you have a cold?" I asked my new co-worker.

"Yes, I'm afraid so."

Being reasonably paranoid, I said, "Please stay away from me." I didn't relish the competition or catching her germs!

For the rest of the day, we kept our distance and only spoke when business necessitated conversation.

Margo was beautiful. She had gorgeous, expressive green eyes, a flawless olive complexion, thick brown hair, and a trim figure. She was also quite a bit younger than I. Those were enough reasons not to like her. This is not good, I thought of my paranoia. I will have to work harder at being civil.

As it turned out, I didn't have to "work" at it one bit.

The next morning, Margo said to me, "I don't really have a cold; I'm sure it's my allergy."

As the day proceeded, we learned each other's history, as her interests, intelligence, humor, and kindness surfaced. We were kindred spirits.

Margo and I had worked together for only a week, when one morning, I opened my personal drawer and found it filled with Godiva chocolates, Godiva cookies, a piece of chocolate cake, and a greeting card infused with heartfelt hand-written birthday wishes. She learned of my birthday from the monthly list posted on the employee entrance bulletin board.

Many bay mates fight over sales and retail trivia. Margo and I also fought over sales, but in a perverse way. We manipulated sales for the other, instead of claiming them for ourselves. I looked forward to coming to work with the "gift box" that was Margo.

We had many moments of hilarious conversations and silliness. We discussed the merits of chocolate ice cream with a mustard sardine topping. I didn't find it all that funny, but Margo shook with laughter and landed on the floor behind the counter.

Margo stayed with Clarins for a year, but she had a string of advanced degrees and desired work in the educational field. She was too highly educated and talented to shake and quake at Dillard's. She ultimately landed a position in special education.

A great gift for her. I was sorry to see her go.

Unflattering in Green

I immediately felt threatened by Lynn when she arrived at the Clarins counter. It was obvious that I was no match for her sales experience, intelligence, and resourcefulness. If that wasn't enough, she was also an exotic Asian beauty, even in the frumpy Clarins uniform. She made all the correct moves at the counter, and the new customers gravitated to Lynn.

Studies have shown that people are more attracted to flashy, good-looking, or interesting looking people than to those who are considered plain. Attraction also increases for individuals who wear bright colors, such as red, or even bright lipsticks. It is human nature.

Although I believed myself to be the No. 1 salesperson in the universe, that certainty vanished when I worked with Lynn. One day, she caught me staring at her. "What's the matter, Marlit?"

I wanted to say, Just leave, Sweetie! Move on!

Instead, I said, "That was a great sale you just had."

I gave myself a lecture: Why are you so disturbed over some silly sale? This isn't your life, you know. But it *was* my life – at least, for that day, for the reality of that moment.

When compliments and high sales figures were announced at the morning and department meetings, or on the store P.A., Lynn's name came up frequently.

Initially, Lynn was cool and distant, and my behavior towards her was similar. I mentioned one day that I collect antique Imari, Japanese porcelain. The dominant colors are brick red and cobalt blue, and the shapes are charming. Modern Imari reproductions look tacky.

Lynn was impressed at this disclosure. I also told her that I had a Korean wedding chest in which I store bedding. Her eyes lit up. Her coldness thawed and morphed into a warm friendliness. I could not help but respond favorably to the "new" Lynn. I mentioned my collection of miniature fragrance bottles, and to my surprise, Lynn collected them as well. From her description, her collection was six times the size of mine! She gave me a generous amount of her doubles.

The hidden layers of Lynn's persona peeled away. Even though I discovered she was an all-around terrific person, working with her wasn't much fun for me.

After several months with Clarins, she was offered a position in the legal profession. She turned it down in favor of her husband's proposal to work for him at one of his beauty salons.

Lynn promised me complimentary beauty treatments at the salon – hair, nails and spa. I did appreciate the gesture, however, my guilt over resenting her precluded my cashing in on her kind offer.

Other Counter Challenges

There were times when only one salesperson was present at a busy counter, instead of the usual four or five. While customers waited to be helped, these ambitious associates tried to tie up two or three customers by waiting on them simultaneously. They had perfected their act by denying idle associates from other counters access to the waiting customers. These salespersons preferred that the customers waited excessively or walked away, rather than let an idle co-worker make a sale.

The scenario was unfair to all participants: the customers were not being properly serviced, the available co-workers made no sales figures, and it sure didn't enhance the store's image.

Only Kidding

She was professionally dressed and well groomed when she applied for the cosmetics position. But when Ms. Purity reported for work, she sported fishnet hose, hair extensions, and a see-through blouse. And her water bottle was filled with vodka. Those who were unaware of her daily vodka ritual wondered about her perpetual exuberance. Her first week of employment, after a two-hour lunch, she returned to work, and fueled by alcohol, threw up in the waste basked in front of on-lookers.

The Search is On

It was common practice for "headhunters" from all department stores to visit cosmetics counters and offer a job to employees. It happened to me several times.

Periodically, my account executive and facialists

asked me to find a replacement for Clarins employees who had left. They wanted me to scout around Saks, Nordstrom and Sephora and *whisk the best away.* Since I knew a lot of the ladies, they felt I'd be more successful at finding a candidate. They intimated I had an obligation to help staff the counter.

Why would I want to do that? I much preferred to have the counter to myself, not so much for the sales, but rather for the freedom. Having a co-worker breathing down my neck or joining my conversation with a customer was an irritant. Even if I called a co-worker out on sales interference, they continued the practice on the pretense of wanting to "learn from me."

PROMOTIONS

One year, my cosmetics line was asked to participate in a promotion with an international theme. Clarins chose Asia, partly because I had visited there and had memorabilia that would make an interesting display. We strategically placed fortune cookies on the counter as well as on a small table in front of the counter.

Four giggling elementary school girls repeatedly returned to the counter to swipe fortune cookies. Was it the fortunes inside the cookies or the cookies themselves that so delighted the girls? I told them that if they brought their mothers (who were elsewhere in the store) I would give each girl a handful of cookies.

Within minutes, two ladies strolled over along with the girls. Both mothers signed up for a facial and each girl received their promised handful of fortune cookies.

Bring on the Men

The introduction of the Clarins men's line prompted expectations of increased sales. Unfortunately these expectations were dashed. Although the products themselves lived up to the excellent Clarins quality, the already established men's lines in the fragrance department had the customers locked in. Women who purchased Clarins men's products at the same time they made their own purchases turned out to be the best customers.

There were a few men who favored Clarins…and not just for fragrances. Some claimed they wanted to buy makeup for a gift, or for a "friend." Some claimed to be in show business and needed stage makeup. And

then there were those who felt no need to hide their...
"Fabulousness." They knew exactly what they wanted
and didn't hesitate to apply colors on their faces at my
counter. I enjoyed working with them.

One guy in particular asked me to apply colors –
the whole enchilada – foundation, eye colors, blush and
even a soft-colored lip glaze. He had a handsome face and
powerful build. I felt good about the color application.
He thought otherwise.

"Just bring me the cleanser and toner," he ordered
as he removed my masterpiece. "I can do a lot better,"
he said with a mischievous twinkle of good humor. But
his "work of art" didn't impress me; he painted his face
theatrically. And then he purchased all the colors *he*
had used.

Good enough.

Chocolate Madness

Once, as a promotion, a menopausal creature was
handing out Godiva chocolate samples to customers.
I approached her and politely asked for a sample. She
refused my request and flat out told me, "Employees
are not included in the give-away." So I grabbed a piece
of chocolate and walked away. Other employees tried
to follow my act, but she got hot flashes so they were
intimidated.

We knew that eventually she would have to
replenish her supply and so one of the gals followed her
to her hiding place. The co-worker located the stash and
we no longer had to beg for a piece of chocolate.

The Holiday That Wasn't

The Memorial Day holiday was a bone of contention for employees. Dillard's does not recognize Memorial Day. Why were we surprised? The Arkansas-based chain had barely accepted the fact that the South lost the Civil War. Employees were not paid time-and-a-half on this national holiday, however, promotional advertising appeared in the newspapers on days preceding Memorial Day.

Dillard's did make a concession and hosted a hot dog picnic during lunch break, which was served on the loading dock.

Nighty Night

To promote a new nighttime treatment, cosmetics associates were instructed to wear pajamas during business hours. "Really? Is a customer going to plunk down money for a night cream because the salesperson is in pajamas?" I complained. I ignored the directive. I don't look devastating in pajamas.

A few misguided ladies complied. Some even wore sleep hats, curlers in their hair, and slippers. What an absurd scene!

What trumped it was a Lancôme associate taking a nap in a reclining chair in the facial room, curled up in her red pajamas.

TATTLE TALES

Power Failure

During a winter power failure, all mall stores including Saks and Nordstrom closed. You guessed it! Dillard's remained open for several hours, operating with dimmed lights. Without power, we couldn't even use the registers.

I didn't mind, since we were getting paid for doing nothing. Besides, I look better in the dark.

It was illegal to keep employees under these conditions, and once the executives were apprised of this fact, they ultimately closed the store.

The next day, the store was still experiencing a total power outage. All store entrances were locked, except for one employee entrance. Clearly, this was a fire hazard violation: about 300 employees and only one door that could be used! The employees responded with complaints and ridicule directed at Dillard's. Finally, an employee called the Beachwood Fire Department to inform them of Dillard's lack of compliance. The officers would be on their way.

Half-jokingly, I told the Cosmetics Queens of the possibility of a T.V. crew arriving and to be prepared. They wasted no time, and after a scramble for makeup and mirrors, were camera ready.

Within minutes, two fire marshals appeared, and in just as many minutes the loudspeaker announced the store was closed.

Enough

A lady in her seventies, well groomed and dressed to the nines, arrived for her usual brouhaha. As always, she carried a bag filled with cosmetics and asked for a store credit. The colors "didn't match," she always said. She asked for a complete color makeover, after which she purchased the *same cosmetics* that she had just returned. This one-act drama was performed monthly and at each visit, she let the associates know that they were just salesgirls.

Finally, Saks sent her a letter asking what was the problem and if there was something the staff was doing wrong?

The visits stopped.

The Flower Incident

Working at a department store cosmetics counter is not for the feint of heart.

Once, when our counter attained high sales for a promotion, the Clarins staff sent us flowers to show their appreciation. Two men delivered the reward. One of the men, looking unkept, maybe in his forties lingered and asked me if I knew Carol, a fragrance spritzer.

"Boy, she's beautiful," he said. "Then again you're not so bad yourself. I'm going to kiss you." As he lunged toward me, he grabbed my arms with an iron grip. I screamed, "Get the hell out of here!" My scream prompted a fast getaway.

I was shaken to the core and just cried. A co-worker observed this sorry scene, and as she examined my bruised arms, advised me to immediately report this to the operations manager. The greeting card attached to the flowers identified the flower shop. Intuitively, I decided to do nothing. I reasoned that if the pervert were reprimanded or dismissed from his job, he might want to retaliate, and he knew where to find me.

My husband supported my decision and picked me up after work a short time afterward.

The flower incident left me uneasy and induced me to change my hairstyle and makeup. This so-called *disguise* was not the solution, but strangely, it comforted me. Still, the flower guy caused me to think, *I must look pretty good for him to want to kiss me.* I admit, it provoked some looks into the mirror.

I encountered other retail hazards besides the mentally deficient flower deliverer. Working in a retail environment brought me face to face with the seductive side of consumerism.

The cosmetics department associates loved to parade their latest acquisitions - clothing, jewelry, purses and shoes. Of course, I also had to have the retail booty. That's what commission checks were for.

Children of the Counter

It's astonishing – each and every employee or ex-employee who schlepped her baby to the store had given birth to a *wunderkind*. When mama and baby arrived, the employees gathered around the progeny and shamelessly gushed. They could barely contain themselves, gasping "Oh, how cute, oh, how precious, how adorable."

The super moms gave exhaustive details of the daily routine, from the time the baby awakened until it went to bed in the evening. More employee shrieks of delight, as they were then exposed to a monologue of painful details of the *birth*.

Did the employees feel they were candidates for sainthood, since they so clearly demonstrated their love for babies?

When the babies became toddlers and were brought in for *Show and Tell*, the mothers coaxed their offspring to perform tricks: "Make by-by. How big is the baby? Throw a kiss."

The little puppets performed, as the employees had simultaneous orgasms.

One's Born Every Minute

A well-dressed woman in her forties approached my counter and fussed with her makeup and hair as she looked in the mirror. I asked her if I could be of any help. She declined my offer.

"There's a rule at the Clarins counter that if you use the mirror, you must make a purchase." I cheerfully told her.

"That's not fair!" She said. "There are no signs."

"I agree with you: There should be signs to inform the customers," I said craftily. "However, Clarins has so many wonderful products, I'm sure you'll find something to purchase."

I glanced at my co-worker, who witnessed the absurd scene and valiantly tried to suppress her emotions. I didn't want to torture the customer any longer, and also, I was unable to hold back my own laugher, so I confessed.

"You were kidding all the time?" she gasped, and relieved, turned back to the mirror.

Looking for Love

While standing in front of my counter as the "idle co-worker," I recalled waiting in line at a diner and overhearing two men discuss women:

"To find good-looking women, just go to the cosmetics department in a department store," the first opined.

"Wow, I never thought of that," was the reply.

"Sure, walk right up to a girl, start a conversation, and then ask her out."

Up Front

One Clarins associate had a knack for selling lots of Clarins bust treatment products.

One day, I finally learned her secret. She asked a customer "What are you doing about your décolleté?"

The customer replied, "I've been married for too many years for it to matter; my husband could care less."

"What about your boyfriend?," the Clarins associate asked.

"I'll take it," the customer swiftly replied.

CUSTOMERS

Working with women made me aware of the flaws of my gender. Many of them are intimidated and regress when confronted with their appearance. They are self-conscious and shy and some demonstrate this trait by behaving foolishly.

Conversely, some women approach the counter with an attitude. They feel they are more knowledgeable about skin care than the beauty adviser (perhaps some are). They question every ingredient and aspect of a beauty aid. The customer is entitled to product and general beauty information, but this particular breed carries it to an extreme.

Some have their cell phones glued to their ears and hand you their shopping list and credit card and make no effort at vocal or eye contact. Some are impatient, rude, condescending and in a great hurry.

Do I have to be the fire hydrant for these customers?

****

The song says, "You Gotta Have friends." Well... not in retail!

Friends can be sales saboteurs. Often my friends and acquaintances, when shopping or taking their morning mall walk, eventually found their way to my counter to chat. They didn't get it! I had a job to do and sales numbers to produce. There's no time for chitchat! I also discovered that friends do not good customers make. No offense to my friends, but what I needed were viable customers with long shopping lists.

When friends make a purchase and are dissatisfied, they hesitate to return the items. If they do make a return, I'm more annoyed with them than I would be with other customers. One of these friends, a mall walker, fussed and tried on the same blush on many visits. Girlfriend, get a life and buy the damn blush already! So I discouraged sales with friends.

"You don't want that lipstick do you? The color isn't right for you," I'd say. I didn't want them to feel that they're being taken advantage of. Nor did I want to feel obligated.

****

Not all customers were fashion plates.

A middle-aged woman in a multicolored sleeveless housedress, knee socks and sneakers once stopped at my counter to study skin care ingredients.

"Those are carcinogens, and anyway, I like to be natural and don't believe in using anything."

"Before you leave your home, do you use toothpaste, mouthwash or shampoo?" I asked. "Do you ever use hand cream when your hands get dry? I can smell the fragrance you're wearing."

I justified that skincare, combined with a healthy lifestyle and diet, is necessary for a good complexion and that color suitably applied enhances a woman's looks and self-confidence. Our products are plant-based and highly regarded around the world. Besides, makeup is fun and uplifting and protects the skin. With monotone glibness, she frequently interrupted with her conviction of the superiority of "naturalness."

I explained that I was not aiming for the big

sale, which would only backfire, but rather I wanted the customers to have a positive experience so they would keep coming back. She still felt "natural" was the way to go, but she "might come back."

"I think you're wearing too much makeup," she said and left.

****

One customer made my day when she decided it was time to change cosmetics lines because she was *out of everything, and wanted to start from scratch.* It didn't get much better than that!

****

"Good morning, do you have any questions? Is there something I can do for you?" I asked the full-figured middle-aged matron as she glanced at the makeup colors. Her neck made a ninety-degree turn as she looked around the cosmetics department.

"Oh, look at all the beautiful women in this department," she exclaimed. "They're so beautiful."

"What about me?" I fished.

"No, not you. You're not beautiful." she answered.

That was a confidence booster. I guess I asked for it.

In the end, I sold her almost the entire treatment and color line. Sweet revenge.

****

I asked a customer standing near my counter, whom I had helped numerous times, if she would like to sign up for a facial.

She screamed at me, "How dare you. You're harassing me. My nerves, my nerves!"

"I'm so sorry," I apologized. "I didn't mean to upset you."

"Well, you did upset me and you're not getting away with it!" She stalked off.

Later that day, I was called into the store manager's office to explain myself. How on earth could I have thought it appropriate to offer a customer a free service?

Both the manager and I concluded that the hysterical lady probably forgot to take her meds.

****

An elderly gentleman approached me, asking for directions to the bathroom. I granted his request, but not without asking, "Would you like to surprise your wife or girlfriend with this wonderful fragrance?"

"I don't have a wife and I don't have a girlfriend," he answered. "But did you hear the one about the brooms?"

"No, I didn't hear the one about the brooms."

"Here it is," he continued. "A female broom told the male broom that she was pregnant. How could that be, the male broom wanted to know, we haven't even swept together."

No sale, but he made my day.

****

Much energy went into a forty-five minute color makeover for a woman in her forties. Her perfume was mixed with perspiration and I held my breath as I worked on a new look she requested. She repeatedly cleared her throat.

When finished, she said, "I don't need anything – I just bought a whole bunch of stuff from Origins," as she coughed in my face and left.

✶✶✶✶

"Oh, my G-d… I'm like… That blush is awesome! I'm hyperventilating!"

No, this was not a teenager in pink and glitter, but a woman whom I judged to be in her forties. She was enthralled by our new blush that featured three colors within a beautifully packaged mirrored compact. I showed her how to achieve a subtle finish by sweeping the makeup brush over three shades.

"Let's pick out a combination of colors that would flatter your skin," I suggested.

"No, That's O.K."

And she walked away.

✶✶✶✶

Tanya got her values from a fashion magazine, where image was more revered than substance. I introduced Clarins treatments to her and explained how to expediently use the beauty aids to comfortably fit into her lifestyle. Before she left, I supplied her with an ample amount of samples and my business card. I followed up by calling her at home to see if she needed more information, sent her thank-you notes after purchases (which were substantial) and lavishly pampered her.

One day, Tanya arrived at my counter with the in-store personal shopper. The personal shoppers tormented (unintentionally) associates throughout the store by selling items from the associates' departments, earning the commissions on these sales for themselves. They help to expedite the shopping needs of their customers, becoming search engines for the goods. It is a well-conceived and practical service. The personal shoppers most adversely affected the associates in the ladies' designer clothing department, and ill feelings existed between the factions.

The personal shopper who came to my counter with Tanya held a list of skincare products and asked me to get them for "her client." I had no choice but to heed her request, as Tanya gave me a big smile (with lipstick on her teeth) and said, "Hi, Marlit, I just love Clarins."

I had done the groundwork to educate and gently force-feed her into the Clarins embrace. Now, the shopper reaped the benefits. Tanya continued this practice and when new Clarins products came on the marked, the shopper pumped me for information.

Why not, I thought. I like to work for nothing.

****

A young woman asked for an explanation and demonstration of the Clarins dry skincare treatments, so I thoroughly explained the various products. After an enthused sales pitch, she thanked me profusely and apologetically.

"You've been very helpful, but since I have a due bill from Saks, I'll have to get my things there." She added, "I'm really, really, sorry, but I heard that you really know what you're talking about."

Great.

****

A lovely young lady, accompanied by her

boyfriend, wanted to purchase some makeup.

Boyfriend: "I don't like makeup."

Me: "Then don't wear any."

✶✶✶✶

At the start of my sales career, I made many errors, one of which was that any first impression of a customer sometimes proved to be false. To judge people by their appearance can be fatal for sales. A bag-lady look-alike comes to mind.

After spending some time with the disheveled person, I learned that there was more to this woman than a superficial glance revealed. In order to recommend the appropriate items, I tried to coax information from her, as to her skin type and lifestyle. She described her skin and I made my suggestions, being careful not to have dollar signs on my mind. Customers instinctively sense this.

Frantically chewing her gum, she said, "You talk too much, just give me this, this, this and this." I followed her lead, kept my mouth shut, and handed her the products, which added up to a substantial amount. I hesitated to thank her for the sale, for fear of talking too much.

Free Samples

"Do you have any samples?" At Clarins, we had to content ourselves with offering "free samples" instead of "Free Gifts." There was a particular herd of women whose agenda was to milk samples wherever they could. They approached the counter with poised thumb and forefinger. They didn't have to say anything. I got the message. Most were polite, however, some were demanding: "I read in the paper that you have to give me samples." Some weren't even specific as to the type of samples they wanted.

By making the store rounds and collecting as many samples as possible, they hoped to avoid the need for a purchase. That's how some careers are forged. I told them I was out of samples when they exhausted their welcome at my counter. However, they were a determined bunch and stopped by on my off times.

Some Examples of Customer Creativity:

1.   After I supplied a customer with samples, she asked, "Could I have some for my mom and sister?"

2.   "I don't get paid till Friday, and I need some samples to tide me over."

3.   "I'm going on vacation, and I don't want to take those heavy bottles with me – could you give me enough samples to last for three weeks?"

4.   "I'm having a dinner party in my home, and I thought it would be cute to put your samples out with the dinner plates."

****

The sample fiends were often seniors.

There was Edna, who ambulated with her walker. This aroused pity in me – what chance did I have but to become the perfect sucker. She recited the same soliloquy when begging for samples: how much she loved Clarins and how good her skin felt after using the treatments. The problem is, as she put it, was that the samples didn't last long enough. Her son drove her to the mall twice a week, and both times, she showed up at my counter.

During one of her twice-weekly stops, she announced she wouldn't be seeing me anymore because her son was placing her in an assisted living home. She loved coming to the mall and now that treat would end. She was in tears. But Edna recovered quickly enough to ask for a large supply of samples to last her for a long time. I loaded her up as we hugged and said our good-byes.

Two weeks later, as I crouched behind my counter, I stood up and there was Edna. She told me how unhappy she was in her new surroundings, how awful the food tasted, and how she didn't care for the staff. One perk was the periodic mall transportation. She asked me for samples. "You can't possibly be out of samples already. What did you do with them?"

"I gave them to my new friends," She replied.

****

Lillian was a Dillard's retiree. She annoyed me while she was working in the frumpy ladies dresses department. She never made a Clarins purchase, but she was frequently at my counter groveling for samples, before and after retirement. I wondered how she'd feel if I asked her for dress samples.

****

Sonia was a cute, perky little lady, always dressed in the latest trendy fashions. When she browsed with a lady friend, she'd say, "This is the nice lady who always gives me samples." Of course the friend also wanted to "try Clarins."

I was getting fed up with Sonia. She never bought one item, although she wore plenty of makeup. I was tired of hearing about her son a prominent gynecologist.

So, one day, I told Sonia to bring in her son, the doctor to buy her some Clarins products. She simply smiled.

At this point, I no longer supplied Sonia with samples and told her I was out of them.

After my husband and I moved into a four-story condominium apartment building, I stepped into the elevator one day, and was shocked to find cute, perky Sonia. She gave me a welcoming greeting and introduced me to her neighbor: "This is the nice lady who always gave me lots of Clarins samples."

RECONSTRUCTION

Dillard's entered an ambitious major store renovation and expansion in conjunction with the enlargement of the Beachwood Place mall. An additional floor was added to Dillard's and the entire store was remodeled. It was a tremendous undertaking.

The complaint department soon reflected a high level of agitation, and rightfully so. Although plastic sheets to control dust were employed, the effort was not enough. The toxins, dust, and noise level were at times unnerving. All the cosmetics counters were moved to temporary locations, which involved much physical work for everyone. Many employees quit, and I was tempted to follow suit. I reasoned that it was easier to put up with the gross inconvenience than to look for another job. I did not want to abandon my comfort zone, such as it was.

We were fortunate that during this upheaval that Pam was our cosmetics manager. She was a calming force who understood the intricacies and demands of the cosmetics department and was up to the challenge. Her friendly attitude and approachability make her the Cosmetics Queens' favorite manager of all time.

Dillard's made a generous and much appreciated gesture by freezing our salaries for one year. If sales did not reach goals, no incomes were cut. However, if sales exceeded goals, raises still were given.

Our spirits soared after the completion of the renovation. Finally, we were in our new permanent locations. Clarins and the small lines occupied standard, though attractive bays. The mega lines had fancier digs since they paid more.

The Dillard's store had nearly doubled in size when the additional floor was added. Many customers, as well as the employees, preferred the compact size of the store before renovation. Sales for many cosmetics lines and other departments went down. Was it the economy, the new presence of Nordstrom, the remodeling of Saks, the cosmetics newcomer, Sephora in the mall, or the store enlargement? Perhaps it was all of the above.

The new Clarins bay was near the inside mall entrance – a very desirable location. We shared the bay with two other lines, but Clarins corporate wanted us to have a bay to ourselves. It was rumored that Jacque Clarins played golf with a Dillard's executive and soon thereafter, Clarins became the sole occupant of another bay. Business increased immediately.

The shoe department ran parallel to the back of the new Clarins counter. This was a benefit in terms of increased traffic. Another advantage was of a more personal nature. My friend Tom, a shoe salesman, placed shoeboxes on the floor behind my counter – that is, after I had made my selections. By wearing the shoes for a while during working hours, I was able to test them. Try before you buy.

Three Scandinavian beauties were now working my ex-counter. They looked as if they had stepped from a fashion runway – tall, blond, and gorgeous. All spoke with accents. It was a coincidence that brought them to the same bay. None took their job seriously and ultimately they were either fired or quit. The bay was always in a state of excitement, either because of the men who frequently visited, or the antics of the Nordic beauties.

Why were the Scandinavian bay mates always giggling over lipsticks? Was it the color, or the customers who wore those colors, or the way the customers applied the lipsticks? What was so funny?

There they were again, in a conspiratorial huddle. Being inquisitive, or downright nosy – and not being one who wants to miss out on anything, I stopped at the counter. Aha! So that was it. Erika was showing off her artistic talent as she carved phallic shapes out of lipsticks. She told me that she planned to apply the lipsticks on the unsuspecting customers during her makeup demonstrations.

Erika was a fast learner. Although she barely spoke English, she learned to use the "F" bomb exquisitely. One day she stopped at my counter and announced, "I'm leaving this place."

"Why?" I inquired.

"After how they fuck me with pay," she answered.

True to her promise, Erika left Dillard's that week, but not before leaving an ample supply of adulterated lipsticks for her co-workers.

THE SAKS SWITCH

Back when Beachwood Place first opened for business, it included a highly anticipated Saks Fifth Avenue store. Saks always had a certain snob appeal. The store's ambience was not lost on the customers, many of whom dressed up to visit, as they eagerly embraced the seductive and trendy concept.

The cosmetics department generated a huge amount of business, and for the first five years after the store opened, the sales associates were treated royally. It was a glamour job. The dress code did not include uniforms, so the Cosmetics Queens wore the latest fashion trends, and the customers were dazzled. Many even competed with the employees with their attire and exaggerated tales of vacations and shopping triumphs. But some shoppers felt intimidated by the milieu.

The pay and perks were generous, with champagne breakfasts and extravagant gifts. The Christmas parties were lavish and elegant, and best of all, the associates were treated with respect.

Then, the manager from hell arrived on the scene. Incidents were not treated in a business-like fashion, but rather on a personal level. She enjoyed pitting the sales people against each other, and went out of her way to encourage divisiveness. The more the employees fought for the sales, the more she gloried in the departmental dissension. She ruled with the proverbial iron fist. Her methods ultimately backfired, changes took place, and she was dethroned.

My husband and I went to Saks to browse in the men's department. As we looked around, a gentleman approached us asking to be of service. He pointed out a jacket's features and informed us that he was the store manager and was helping out because Saks was temporarily short staffed.

Bernie bragged about my sales career at Dillard's. He told the manager what a terrific sales person I was and wildly exaggerated my accomplishments. He confided to the manager that Saks was his favorite store, and that he would love to see me work there to take advantage of its generous employee discount policy.

Bernie's pitch was successful and the sales manager's interest was piqued. He said he'd be happy to have me interview with the cosmetics sales manager.

I answered, "Not at this time and besides, Saks couldn't afford me."

He quickly replied that, indeed, Saks could afford me and that I should give it a try.

I was disgustingly arrogant. At the time I didn't want to make a change. Nevertheless, I should have shown the manager more respect and given him a more tactful response.

PART-TIME

Having worked several years as a full-time employee for Dillard's, I decided to cut my hours and become a part-timer. I looked forward to the decreased working hours and to the opportunity to work for a different cosmetics company. It would be a welcome challenge and change.

At that time, Clarins hired no part-timers. The cosmetics department manager promised to place me with a busy new line. But Eric, my long-time Clarins boss, had other ideas. He wanted me to stay with Clarins, even as a part-timer.

"Will you continue to be hard-working and conscientious as a part-timer?" he asked.

"Why would you want me to remain with Clarins, if you have to ask that question?" I replied.

I had to step down from being counter manager, though I didn't consider it to be stepping down. Rather, I felt elevated. I no longer wanted the headaches and responsibilities of a counter manager position. However, I often felt like a third-class citizen, out of the loop in the cosmetics department and even at my counter.

When regular customers asked for me, a select few co-workers gleefully informed them of my new schedule by saying I was hardly ever there. Three full days a week, to me, did not translate into *hardly ever there.*

It got back to me that these exaggerated tales of my absence were even being told at the Clarins counters at Saks and Nordstrom in the mall. I suppose I should have been flattered. Even in a whole other store, I was still considered a threat.

After my transition to part-time, Julia became the new Clarins counter manager. My customers continued to deal only with me, which made Julia anxious and aggressive. She felt she had to prove herself.

As an adjunct to selling treatments and colors, I engaged willing customers in meaningful conversations about my son Richard's fourth published book. It had just been released, so I regaled my customers with a monologue on the merits of the book as any mother would. Sales figures don't lie. This obnoxious mother was responsible for helping increase sales of Richard's opus.

Julia was unhappy with my sideline. She made snide remarks about my book-selling endeavors. I admit it was not professional, but what's a mother to do?

Ultimately, she concluded that fighting with me was a no-win battle, and so we joined forces. Not only did she purchase my son's book, but she also asked the mother of the author to autograph it.

NORDSTROM IN CLEVELAND

When Nordstrom opened at Beachwood Place, there was much fanfare, media coverage, and excitement, just as there had been in New York.

I planned to apply for a job, since a visit to Nordstrom in Seattle had impressed me, thanks to the store's first-rate customer service, upscale merchandise, and attractiveness. I borrowed the library book, *The Nordstrom Way,* which stressed the premium the store put on quality service and Nordstrom's high expectations of its employees. The book cautioned job seekers that Nordstrom is a tough place to work, which made me want the job even more!

It soon became apparent that many other Dillard's employees had the same idea.

A cosmetics job fair, which included Nordstrom, was taking place at a nearby hotel. It took me 20 minutes to apply my makeup to look "natural." (The older I get, the longer it takes me to look "natural") As I entered the huge banquet room, I glanced at the tables manned by account executives from many cosmetics companies. I did a double-take when I spotted the Clarins account executive at one of the tables. We made eye contact, and I thought *my goose is cooked.* What could I do, but to walk directly to her table? I had to think fast, so I told her that I would like to remain with Clarins, however, at Nordstrom instead of Dillard's, even though the truth was that I was open to any quality cosmetics line.

Without hesitation, she told me the job was mine as far as she was concerned and that she would highly recommend me to the Nordstrom cosmetics manager.

But then she advised me I'd be better off staying at Dillard's, since I would have the freedom, flexibility and income that I had come to enjoy and expect.

The Nordstrom manager was anxious to hire me after the favorable recommendation by the Clarins executive. The Nordstrom cosmetics department required a four-day or more workweek, meaning the end of my part-time, three-day week. I was not willing to give up that extra day, so I turned down the position. It turned out to be the right decision.

Later, I learned that Nordstrom deliberately over-hired – a tactic often used during the opening of new branches. The newly hired employees worked hard to help assemble and stock the new store. After the initial opening excitement and the large crowds dissipated, a high percentage of employees were terminated. It was a hardship for many who had left their previous jobs for the privilege of working for Nordies.

A Nordstrom Story:

"You can't park here," the young attendant said, as I was halfway into a parking space in the Nordstrom covered garage area.

"Why not?" I asked.

"This is Nordstrom valet parking. Can't you see the signs?"

"Well, there's no sign where I'm parked."

"Someone must have ripped off the sign. You can't park here."

I screeched, "I'm now in this spot and I'm staying!"

My husband, Bernie, who was a passenger in the car, enjoyed the performance and took delight in my defiance. Before I found my parking spot, I had driven around the outdoor parking lot several times without finding a space.

Once inside Nordstrom, Bernie and I sat down in the men's shoe department to shop for sneakers, and Bernie casually mentioned the parking incident to the shoe clerk.

Oh, no! I recognized the store manager as she walked toward us. I thought I must be in trouble because of the garage incident. The snippy kid had probably reported me.

The young, beautiful, and charming manager apologized for our unpleasant parking experience and handed us four cards. They were for complimentary dinners and drinks at Nordstrom restaurant and coffee shop. We didn't expect this!

It was an example of how Nordstrom turned a negative experience into a positive one, emphasizing customer service and validating their reputation. Even though it wouldn't have been the right place to work, it was a great place to shop.

That very evening, Bernie and I thoroughly enjoyed dinner and beverages at their restaurant.

HIGH ALERT

The Clarins account executive and facialist were a-twitter. The big guns from New York were scheduled to visit.

We received our directives: Have the counter sparkling clean, rearrange the cases, be dressed in proper uniform with no jewelry (other than small earrings), and show enthusiasm. Also we should stand outside the counter and hold a product in our hand. We looked like bookends in our red uniform dresses.

We prepared and anticipated for a month, but when the big day arrived, the execs were a no show.

When executives from Clarins *did* finally appear at my counter and gave me instructions on how to perform tasks in the prescribed manner, I smiled and nodded in agreement. Then, after they left, I did what I felt was best for business.

The execs had a fetish for moving testing units, props, stands and merchandise. Clarins wanted uniformity among the stores, which was understandable, but not always practical. Each area had it's own distinctive flavor. As soon as the visitors left and were out of sight, I immediately moved everything back.

Eric had flown in from New York. He gave me a warm greeting and the perfunctory kiss. After the inspection, I took Eric aside and asked, "How is Clarins doing at Bloomingdale's in New York?"

"I don't want to talk about it," he said stiffly.

Of course he didn't, and I knew why. My Bloomingdale's friends and I had kept in touch, and they apprised me of the Clarins situation. Sales were down since I left, and the current Clarins associates were not altogether competent.

UNWELCOME WELCOME

Eric and I enjoyed a satisfying chat whenever he flew in from New York. On this particular trip, he walked straight to my counter from the store manager's office with a determined gait.

Oh, oh, he looks unhappy, I thought.

There was no greeting. He blurted out, "Do you know how much money you're making?"

Indeed I did, especially since I'd just gotten a raise.

"Do you know that you are being paid a very high wage?" he continued.

Eric discovered that, at one point, my income was higher than the facialists' and he was even more astonished to learn that my income surpassed many of the department managers' income.

That year, I had been on fire. My commissions, overrides and bonuses had added up. If Eric was waiting for an apology, none would be forthcoming. I didn't understand Eric's logic. After all, I brought in money for Clarins.

My income situation was not left unnoticed by Dillard's. At my next evaluation, I was given new and impossible sales goals.

NEW MINDSET

After each inventory, I made a silent vow to leave Dillard's. This time, I meant it. I was ready to follow the herd and head for the Promised Land. I had previously turned down the Nordstrom position, and had acted rudely with the Saks store manager when he offered me a job, but this time I felt desperate to make a change.

There was more to my unrest than anxiety about inventory: Three months before my upcoming review, I realized my sales had taken a nosedive, and if I couldn't raise my numbers, a pay cut would be in my future.

The future was now.

Gregg, the cosmetics manager who was so high on himself, summoned me for a meeting. "I guess you know that you didn't reach your goal and that you're getting a 10% cut in pay.

I had been in the cosmetics trenches for over sixteen years and consistently gave it my all. I wanted to cry – not so much for the pay cut (which was substantial and which I didn't take lightly), but rather for the indifferent and unfeeling treatment I received from Gregg.

I fiercely defended my position – being saddled with impossible sales goals. I knew it was a losing battle, but why let Gregg off easily?

"It's the economy, stupid," I shot at Gregg, and walked out of the room.

Such was my frame of mind when I made an appointment with the Saks cosmetics manager. This time, I had a more humble attitude than I did several years ago.

When I walked through Saks and saw so many former Dillard's employees who now worked there, I questioned if indeed I was in the Saks store.

The interview went well, and the manager was ready to hire me, but asked for my permission to speak with my Clarins account executive. She was against the idea of me moving to Clarins at Saks. I don't know the reason she gave the manager. My guess: She did not want to disturb the status quo at Dillard's. She had more than once told me that she wished she could clone me because of my sales performance, and she had tried to convince me of the advantage of staying with Dillard's.

Instead of actively pursuing a Saks cosmetics position with another line, I decided to stay with Dillard's. But not for long.

I had planned to get out of retail altogether by the following year. If I had gotten the Saks job, it would have been only a brief interlude before my "retirement."

The much-heralded opening of Nordstrom and Sephora resulted in reduced sales for Saks and Dillard's. Strict and often unrealistic goals were imposed on my fellow Rouge Hags.

It was time to leave the counter.

AUF WIEDERSEHN

After I put away my makeup brushes and turned in that horrible crimson Clarins uniform, I reflected on my career in the beauty business.

I loved working at Bloomingdale's. Having worked at Dillard's and *not* loving it, what compelled me to stay for ten years?

Although not the income of a Wall Street CEO, my pay was excellent for the position I held. The sense of camaraderie was also a powerful incentive to stay. The ambience and community of beauty culture was uplifting, giving me a sense of belonging and contributing.

I also lived within walking distance of the mall.

Of course, I could have had these perks in many other positions or other stores. It is easy to justify and rationalize one's actions. There is a "time and season for everything," and so it was time for me to say good-bye, again, but this time with finality.

Good-bye to retail. Good-bye to skin care and cosmetics. Good-bye to co-workers, customers, managers, and executives. Good-bye to the fun, craziness, disappointments, politics, lunch and dinner breaks, car-parking games, and to the challenges. Good-bye to a world that captured my mind and heart for many years.

Good-bye, Rouge Hags, and thanks for the ride.

A feeling of relief as well as loss engulfed me after my professional divorce from Dillard's. It prompted me to go "out in the field" to interview my fellow beauty advisers and fragrance models. It occurred to me that our stories needed to be told. Plus it would be therapeutic.

I presumed their experiences would mirror my own. As it turned out, some of their tales were quite unique and different from mine. I intended to ferret out the unusual situations and customers. My contacts delivered. The ladies were in true form as only the cosmetics and fragrance ladies can be – laughing uproariously as they shared anecdotes.

Interacting with the Rouge Hags was nostalgic and bittersweet. As I talked to an employee at a counter next to the Clarins bay, a former customer called out to me.

"Marlit, could you get me my firming cream?"

"I'll be happy to get that for you."

She was aware that I no longer worked for Dillard's, and we were both play-acting. Just the same, I was tempted to get her the cream from behind the counter and ring the sale.

A Little Color

I mined some fabulous tales from my cosmetics cohorts.

I loved this story:

A customer walked up to the Lancôme counter to return a ruined lipstick. There was just a stub left in the tube. The customer had pulled this stunt numerous times.

"Fine," said the counter manager, retrieving a new lipstick of the same color. She opened the new tube as well as the old lipstick and laid them side-by-side. The manager then reached behind the counter, produced a metal nail file and proceeded to cut the new lipstick down to the same size as the old one. She then took a tissue, picked up the cut portion and threw it in the waste basked in front of the customer.

The customer lost it.

****

Another Rouge Hag told of an "old lady" who headed for fragrances, strutting through the cosmetics department in her bright purple coat, purple hat, purple shoes and purple purse. Her outfit matched her poodle's; the pooch was decked out in a purple coat and rhine-stone collar.

The lady wore a dog carrier on her shoulder, in which the doggie was comfortably seated like a queen on a throne.

All eyes, employees as well as customers, were riveted on the hilarious scene.

****

At Sephora, a makeup artist told me that a customer once fell asleep as he applied makeup. So he kept going while she snored away.

****

Many customers feel that Saks is the store to be seen in. Even customers who are unsavory want to be unsavory at Saks.

When returning products they pull the switch act, claiming they are allergic to the cream or that their faces broke out. Upon inspection, the employee found that the cream in the jar was replaced by a counterfeit and cheaper drugstore cream.

A similar situation: Customers arrive at a cosmetics counter and scoop out the entire contents of a high-priced cream such as La Mer or Cle de Peau. They carry the cream in their hands into the mall, where they then place the cream into their own jars.

****

The spritzers, or models as they like to be called, shared with me that customers often mispronounced fragrance names.

A popular fragrance by Givenchy is called YSATIS. It's pronounced, Ee-sah-tees. A gentleman once approached a model and asked her "Do you have itsy-titsy?" It didn't help that he stared at her breasts.

****

A customer asked Chris at the Lauder counter for a makeover. Her overly made-up face was almost scary, and she told Chris she wanted a natural look.

Chris did what she thought the customer wanted.

The customer looked into the mirror and shrieked. She grabbed the makeup brush from Chris's hand and swirled it into an electric blue eye shadow, then applied it to the entire eye contour area. She then placed several layers of foundation on her face. This was followed with the customer's application of the brightest blush and lipstick, black mascara and black eye pencil. All were applied with a heavy hand.

"Now that looks much better," said the delighted customer, and she purchased all of her own selected colors.

This happened during prom season: Two teens, who had appointments with Chris, saw the Technicolor lady leaving and said to Chris, "Can we have somebody else?"

∗∗∗∗

The fragrance, French Connection, United Kingdom, was sold as F.C.U.K. The customers often referred to it intentionally or unintentionally as F.U.C.K. Some shoppers complained about the play on words and the cheeky fragrance was ultimately removed from Nordstrom.

∗∗∗∗

Some customers like to spray themselves all over – their neck, behind the ears, their arms, behind the knees. A few fragrance lovers just want to take a bath with the stuff. After spraying themselves all over, they headed south, lifted up their skirts or dresses and sprayed some more.

∗∗∗∗

After selecting a fragrance, one customer asked to have it gift-wrapped. The fragrance model complied and handed the wrapped fragrance to the shopper.

The shopper tore off the ribbon and wrapping paper and crushed it into a ball. She then threw the paper ball into the fragrance model's face, saying, "I can do a better job than this."

∗∗∗∗

A cross-dresser, who was also a member of the military, wanted Danielle to give him a makeover in a private room. Danielle freaked out and didn't want to be alone with a stranger. He wore a stuffed bra under his clothes. (What G-d has forgotten, he stuffed with cotton). He removed a wig from his pocket and placed it on his head. He looked very masculine, and Danielle tried hard not to look "down there" – but there it was – the "sergeant" was standing at attention.

It was the fastest makeup application Danielle ever pulled off.

****

Before leaving the chair, a customer asked the makeup artist, "Did you throw water on me? I feel something wet on the chair. You must have thrown liquid on me."

The makeup artist looked perplexed, as the customer got off the chair and walked away.

She left behind a dripping puddle. Maybe she couldn't hold it.

****

A customer thanked Danielle for the makeover and for her help. Then she said, "This would be a great job for my niece. What kind of training do you need? She's good with this kind of stuff. She's not so bright."

P.S. Danielle has a bachelor of fine arts, plus a master's degree in art history.

****

Robyn, who has been in the beauty business for over twenty years, is not only an excellent makeup artist, but also an astute business woman and hustler. She approached the men who were near her counter and asked them if she could be of help with any gift ideas. The reply often was, "No thank you." She followed them

with her voice and said, "You could've gone home a hero."
It often worked.

Dena recalled her first working day in cosmetics.

She noticed an elderly man carrying a briefcase.
He was shabbily dressed, had dirty hair, a dirty face and
wore dirty torn sneakers. To Dena's surprise, the man
walked directly to her and purchased twelve bottles of
Chanel No.5. He then opened his torn briefcase. It was
filled with $100 bills.

****

Dena, along with her two co-workers, arrived
at a nursing home where they greeted the wheelchair
brigade. The cosmetics associates applied lipstick, blush
and powder, as they talked to the women. Most residents
did not respond to their chatter.

Dena selected a woman who, according to the
nurses, hadn't communicated with anyone for months.
She introduced herself and talked to the woman as she
applied powder and blush. Still there was no response.
Then Dena said to her, "I'm now going to put lipstick on
you." The resident perked up, sat up straight and pursed
her lips. The nurses were incredulous. Dena's eyes welled
up with tears as she told me this story.

We concluded that no matter the age or
circumstance, most women just want to look good.

I have always had a soft spot in my heart for Eric, and after my departure from Dillard's, he called to chat. He asked if I could do him a favor and keep an eye on a new Clarins employee at Dillard's. I was dumbfounded and could only mumble something incoherent. To me, this request was beyond rational, since I was now a former employee.

When I recovered from Eric's absurd suggestion, I mentioned that I was in the process of writing a book about my past experiences in the retail business as a beauty consultant. I told him that Çlarins and he personally are represented in the book. That piqued his interest.

"I want you to send me the manuscript before showing it to a publisher," Eric ordered. I didn't think this was a good idea, and told him so. I explained to him the difficulty of having a book published, however, should I be that fortunate, he could go to the bookstore and buy one!